What others are saying about this book:

"…excellent job blending personal insight, technical information, and helpful hints in a balanced way."

 **W9-DEW-706**

"…a caring style…"

" 100% support for kids and parents!"

"For moms, dads, teachers; anybody who deals with kids will learn a few pointers from this book."

"This mom knows and she shares what she knows without judgment."

"Sound advice, lots of options, and a joy to read."

"Ms. Miller may not be a medical or mental health professional, but she sure is a *Doctor Mom*."

"I'll be recommending to my clients…"

"Reading this book is almost like calling my best friend for advice."

Your Child Needs A Champion…
So you can be your child's champion, too!

Your Child Needs A Champion

Mastering the A.D.D. Challenge by Making the Right Choices

Jane Miller

JMA Publications
A Division of Miller & Associates

Copyright information continued on page 203.

Library of Congress Catalog Card Number: 97-93086

Library Data
Miller, Jane
        Your Child Needs A Champion Mastering the A.D.D. Challenge by Making the Right Choices / Jane Miller - 1st Ed.

ISBN # 0-9658190-0-0

1. Attention Deficit Disorder- 2. Parenting - 3. Child
    Development
I. Miller, Jane 1961-.
II. Title

This reference is based on the author's personal experience with and research of A.D.D. Contents are not intended to replace medical and/or psychological diagnosis or treatment of A.D.D. Readers should consult a qualified physician or health care professional in matters related to physical and mental health. This reference is not to be considered as medical advice.

Printed in the United States of America
First Edition

For Cassie and Joey

CONTENTS

(Three, cont.)

WELCOME

You are the only one who can do what's right for your child. You are the only one with enough passion to fight for your child. You are the only one - to be your child's champion.

Sure, you need support from doctors, teachers, therapists, etc., still it's you. You will make the choices and you will master Attention Deficit Disorder (ADD) on behalf of your child. You will also guide others who teach, coach, and help you to raise your child. You, you, you! Seems like a tall order, an almost impossible task. You may be wondering, "Can I do all this?" That's why I've written *Your Child Needs A Champion: Mastering the ADD Challenge by Making the Right Choices* - to help you to believe that you can.

You've made a choice to read more about ADD and I applaud you! Maybe someone has pointed out, rather directly, that your child is a "handful." Perhaps this child you care for is facing academic or social frustration. Discipline problems may be the root of your concerns. In any case, something is disturbing the peace in your lives. You've tried the normal parenting stuff and nothing seems to be working. You're searching for a clue, a plan, anything that might be helpful. You are determined to make a difference in this child's life.

Just who are *you*? You're the nurturer of an ADD child. You may be a mom, a dad, a relative or guardian. Perhaps you're a teacher trying to assist parents or a doctor trying to get a true feel for parents' frustrations. In any case, if you're reading this book, you're someone who cares - someone who cares enough to be a champion for a child.

I too was (am) in this place of exploration and I am pleased to present this reference. It is meant to be an end user's guide, a how-to of sorts. I hope you'll write notes in the margins, share it with your family, and loan it out repeatedly so that others may seek its assistance. It's only a book, but through it may you find assistance and inspiration as you master the ADD challenge on behalf of your child(ren).

Lastly, thank you for picking up this book. When you have read it and it is helpful, your efforts will have meant so much to a child in your life, and to me. Keep championing!

1

WHY YOU SHOULD READ THIS BOOK

What's Out There Already on ADD?

In searching for a publisher for this book, I received a number of responses from editors who noted that the market was already overflowing with books on the subject of Attention Deficit Disorder (ADD[1]). Thinking I must have missed that one book that would talk to me in plain language while suggesting a variety of practical advice, I took another look at the library and in local and national bookstore chains. No, I saw that the same books were still there, those written by doctors, psychologists, counselors and clinicians of all types. Featured were books by authors brandishing M.D.s Ph.D.s, M.Ed.s and one with an R.P.N. But, there were none written by an M.O.M. One book highlighted its inclusion of the true story of an ADD child written by his parent. But, I still felt that there was room for at least one (or two) more helpful books on ADD.

---

[1] ADD is meant to include any of the Attention Deficit/Hyperactivity disorders; hyperactive/impulsive type, inattentive type, or combination type.

Look, I have read a dozen books and hundreds of articles about ADD. Yet, in most of my reading I have felt alone as I face this disorder for the benefit of my children and family. Even the literature developed by support groups, well loaded with facts, left me without a clear idea of what to do next. I had questions about how to design and implement an appropriate action plan for my child. I wondered just how much I could interface with my child's teacher without seeming overbearing. Too, it seemed as if each title was the last word on the subject. How would I know if I had found the thing that was best for my child? And if I found something that seemed to work, was my job finished? I wondered what was still being studied and if there were any new theories. The authors were very thorough at providing explanations of ADD, if the reader could sift through the technical, medical and psychological terminology. (What is a neurotransmitter, anyway?) Most authors were very careful to provide only the accepted solutions for treating my child. However, as I read through their facts, figures and suggestions, I couldn't help wondering if their opinions would be different if they were speaking about their own children. And, would they administer the same treatment for their own kids? Would they settle for the standard RX - behavior modification plus prescription medication? Or would they, like you and me, have the initiative to question the accepted theories and treatments in search of the best situation for our children?

Don't get me wrong, each new piece I read helps me along my journey of dealing with my family's ADD challenges. Yes, family. If someone in the household has ADD, the whole family is challenged as well. Most helping professionals that I have come across in my quest have been sincere enough in their judgments and advice. Still, I questioned their advice because unless they have a child of their own affected by ADD, how could they know? How could they; doctors, psychologists, pharmacists, and so on, truly understand the ADD child and her challenges and frustrations. Sympathize maybe, know how we feel, they could not. This is what I kept searching for in my reading. I wanted someone to say, "Hey, this is what you might be facing today and tomorrow, so here is something you might try. Oh, and did anyone ever say thus and so to you? Yeah, me too."

So if you're just looking for some raw information about ADD with some case histories and theory thrown in, the market has many titles to offer. I list some in the back of the book in the resource section. On the other hand, if you need that information in plain language presented with real understanding - empathy- you've picked up the right book.

What Makes This Book Different

I'm the mother of two ADD children. No, I'm not looking for pity. While I fulfill many roles in my life, none is as important to me as the job of parenting my kids. No other role is as difficult either, or as fulfilling when it goes well. Adding the challenges of ADD to our lives quite frankly has created havoc, chaos and a general state of frenzy in the Miller household. In my quest to improve the situation, I've read many how-to, parenting, and self help books. While the messages made sense to me and were indeed well presented, somehow the advice just never worked for us. I'd try and try and try harder still, but there was always some obstacle to our success. The obstacle, and maybe you've faced it too, was that the authors did not take into consideration the implications of ADD in the lives of those they were trying to help. Why would any author for such a small percentage of her readership? Well, I did! For you, and for me.

Your Child Needs A Champion was written with the haze of ADD all around me. Its never ending supply of surprises and obstacles certainly helped to keep the focus of these pages on a parent's everyday need for guidance. For example, while rushing to meet a deadline for my editor one week, there was a huge crash in the bathroom. My six-year-old, Joey, had leapt (impulsively) onto the shower rod sending both him and the rod into the tub (surprise). At the same time, my eight-year-old, Cassie, sat staring at a blank homework page (obstacle) forty minutes after she began (no surprise). Things in the Miller home aren't perfect. Gees, they're not even ordinary. So, I have a fair idea of what it can be like at your house, and when I suggest yet another positive discipline scheme, I'll be skeptical right along with you. I may even preface such things with a chuckle or two. Most how-to books strive to provide helpful information, and we are free to judge the usefulness of that information. I have taken pains to provide a variety of details on ADD, even though I may not wholly agree with it all. But what doesn't work for my family might work for yours, so feel free to form your own opinion. You will find practical easy to follow direction for dealing with ADD everyday.

Having my own ADD "subjects" to study and test certainly helps to create a personal tone for this book. But, in addition to the presence of ADD in my life, this book is different because of its purpose. While that purpose includes informing, its foremost goal is to provide a level of consumerism. Now that doesn't mean where to shop for ADD related goods. It does mean that we as parents or guardians must continue to look for the best possible blend of strategies, treatments and cures for our children faced with ADD. It means that we should not, we must not, hand over the responsibility of raising and helping our children to anyone else.

This book is designed to help you maintain the control that society sometimes wants to take away "for the sake of your child."

And this book is different because it recognizes the whole you. You are strong as you fight for the best instruction for your child. You are understanding as you listen to your child and ignore judgments from others. And, you are angry, confused, and filled with guilt. You are one needing time for yourself, time to reflect, space to consider. I know this to be true. In these pages you will find support in the words and stories of others dealing with ADD. These are not typical case histories but comments, anecdotes and insights from people just like you. The things they share serve to support and enlighten you.

Who Should Read This Book

This book is especially for you, the nurturer of an ADD child. Whether you are a mom or dad, grandparent, sibling, caregiver or guardian, you will find in these pages support and guidance that can help. In most cases I refer to the parent of the ADD child but only for ease of reading. If you're concerned about a child, the term "parent" is meant to be you no matter what your role. You probably began your search for help like many parents do. Maybe you feel that you've lost control with your child. Other people raise an eyebrow towards you and your child all too often. Perhaps it's yet another note home from teacher outlining your child's latest act. You're not alone. Here we are, trying to do all the right things, giving our hearts and souls to our kids and look! Look what has happened. Our kids are in trouble and we've turned into parenting wimps. Well, it may not necessarily be that bad, my dear parent. Being at wit's end may just be the first clue encouraging you to reach out for help.

You should also read this book if you've heard or read about ADD courtesy of the media. It seems that 1995 had to be the year that the media declared war on ADD, but not in a helpful way. Story after story seemed to portray ADD as merely a fad. It's a shame really, many of the reports concluded that there is no such disorder, and then pointed to a cure of "better parenting" of these "bratty" children. The US Department of Education reviewed articles published within the last few years about kids with disabilities. The findings are grim - articles ran three to one against the kids. Three to one against the kids! Even through all the hype, you may have picked up a clue that this thing may be real, that ADD might be the thing that is troubling your child. If so, congratulations on looking past judgments and thinking about your child.

Perhaps your child's trouble seems more subtle than what you think accounts for a "real" ADD diagnosis. Maybe her teacher notices your child becomes distracted at times. Is this cause to worry? How can you figure out the clues? This book provides direction to help you on your quest. Many times an observant teacher will suggest ADD as a possible point of trouble. However, just as often we hear of parents struggling on their own, trying to make sense of a confusing situation. I provide lots of information, clues, current theories, etc. that can help you decide just what to do.

This book is not only for those of us new to ADD. You may have already been struggling for years with ADD. Bravo! Keep reading everything you can. Keep searching for new ways and review old ways that may provide relief for your child. And suggest that your child's pediatrician or counselor do the same. Many times these professionals don't have the time to weed through all the text that's out there. Let them know what you're reading and how it has helped. Others who can gain from reading this book include teachers, coaches, school assistants, and other children's helpers. How often have you wished that others could better understand the challenges our children face? You can help by offering them information such as what's in this book. When Coach can find a way to help Johnny focus his excess energy, the whole team benefits. When Babysitter realizes that the broken toy was not intentional but a result of impulsive behavior, a child's self esteem is protected.

Take The Time To Learn

Be informed. One of your best tactics for facing a society who has been conditioned to think of ADD as just a passing fad, is to be informed. You will be called upon for this knowledge each time you help your child fight for appropriate education, each time you reach out for support and find judgment instead, and each time your child suffers frustration but meets only with criticism. You can meet such criticism with knowledge as your defense. There's no need to apologize to others about your child's behavioral challenges. There is a great need to be by your child's side, supportive and encouraging. Another reason to learn all you can is to rule *out* the possibility of ADD in your child's life. As you read, you may find that your child doesn't seem to exhibit ADD after all. However, you'll still want to make sure by being aware of its characteristics and methods of diagnosis. And, by reading to rule out, you may discover other reasons for certain behaviors and the references where to turn. In trying to formulate a diagnosis for ADD, many clinicians first look for other explanations for hyperactive or inattentive behavior. Illness and anxiety, among other things, can trigger ADD-like behaviors in some children. The frustrations of a learning disability can lead to symptoms typical of ADD as well.

How To Use This Book

You may be wondering why I'm suggesting ways to read this book, after all most of us learned in first grade how to begin at the beginning and read through to the end. That certainly is an approach that will serve some readers. If you're really anxious to find that certain passage that might help you now, feel free. The index should help you locate the topic you're looking for. Do strive to read all the sections as there may be just the right insight waiting to be read. Read to learn and also read for reflection. Ask yourself, "How is this topic reflected in my own life, my child's life?" Read to gain support. Others will be with you in their words and stories. They have shared these stories because they know that you too may be feeling all alone in this fight. Read for a reality check. It's easy to get lost in your struggle and sometimes reviewing some facts can help. Finally, read for peace and read to nurture your soul.

What You'll Find

Chapter Two serves as our ADD primer, worded in everyday language for us everyday parents. What is ADD? What isn't it? What are some clues to look for in your child? I present the most and least obvious traits and characteristics. I discuss how a diagnosis is made, who makes it and what to do with it. I explore the current and historical theories pointing to the causes of ADD, and briefly outline their corresponding treatment. Those treatments and others are then fully discussed in Chapter Four. Clinical professionals may find my primer lacking in the technical mumble jumble typical of their fields of study. If you really need the additional information and confusion, references are listed in the back of the book, help yourself. By the way, who pays for all these professionals? This chapter will give you the guidelines.

In the third chapter we consider the ways we find out about ADD and the ways that we do not. You'll learn about awareness levels including ignorance (an unawareness of ADD), denial (a rejection of the existence of ADD or its affects), exploration (a search to learn about ADD and it's relationship to your child), and acceptance (an attitude that helps to formulate a plan of action, it is not a state of giving up or giving in). These levels of awareness contribute to our action, or inaction, as we move through this process of change. Yes, change. If ADD is indeed a factor in your child's life, and thus your life, you have already seen change or a need for it. You'll be able to recognize where you are in this cycle of awareness.

Chapter Three also provides insight into what can happen if we choose to get stuck in the ignorance or denial levels. By ignoring or denying the effects that ADD can have on our children's abilities, we may be choosing to sentence them to a life time of limited potential. And it's not just a question of academic ability. Some ADD characteristics left untreated, like impulsive behavior or lack of self-control, can lead to physical injury of self or others, experimentation with drugs, or criminal activity such as shoplifting or property damage. The concern is not just so that our child can make straight A's or be picked first for the soccer team. It is a lifelong concern that can affect a child for always. We need to be aware of the horrible things that can happen and do, so that we can help our child strive for better.

As noted, Chapter Four provides further explanation of a variety of treatment methods for helping the ADD child. I discuss what the particular treatment is, and it's pros and cons as reported by numerous sources. You see, just because source A says treatment X isn't proven yet so it's hogwash, we must remember that each child responds in her own way to different treatments. Of course this comes with a caution - never try any treatment method without seeking an opinion from your child's pediatrician. The idea is not to self treat, but to consider many options. These options include nutritional therapy, medication, behavior modification, physical reflex therapy, and others. Some children respond best to a combination of methods. Some methods seek to treat only the effects of ADD, while other methods attempt to move toward a cure. You will find enough information about each to consider them and references to research them further.

It may seem for many of us that the onset of ADD coincides with the beginning of the school years. The structure of the school environment can tend to amplify the characteristics of ADD, even though they have been with your child for most of his young years. Chapter Five focuses on school relationships and skills. We can work to form a partnership between school and home, but sometimes we might face a battlefield if we can't get for our child what he needs to succeed. Your child's own relationship with her teacher is something she will face everyday. So, there's a delicate balance in helping her get appropriate assistance (i.e., testing, remedial help, tutoring) while not becoming a nuisance in your efforts. We'll discuss how to foster a good relationship and how to overcome conflicts that may arise. School days spill over to the home front, especially at homework time. I present a section focusing on learning styles. Different learning styles call for different styles of study skills. Homework hour can be much more pleasant if we adapt the structure to meet the child's learning styles. And, this knowledge will help you talk intelligently to your child's teacher about ways to improve your child's success at school.

If you feel like some days consist of one disappointment after another, you're not alone. What can you do when you're trying your best at parenting, your child is trying, or so seems to be, but even little successes are eluding you? In Chapter Six we take a break from all this serious stuff, as we consider activities outside the ABC's and 123's of a child's life. ADD kids especially need to find success outside the academic environment. You'll learn how to discover your child's special gifts and to celebrate them. See how you can find or create an activity that matches your child's interests and that meets her needs for social, physical or mental stimulation. Oh, but watch out for overload signals in your child. I discuss the need for down time as well.

Most of us have been saturated with how-to parenting messages in the 90's. Society expects us to improve. Even President Clinton of the United States encouraged a refocusing on the family - although his message came across more like blame to me. So we try, and try. But when grades are dropping, sibling fighting is at an all time high, the living room is in a shambles and the dog is hiding under the bed again, our confidence can waver. Chapter Seven focuses on finding a way to instill fundamental principles of behavior in our children. There are many popular discipline approaches based on assertiveness, positive language, reward systems and so on. Other experts insist that a values based approach is the best route - yet it's not a new idea. I take you back to the sixties when Dr. Haim Ginott, since deceased, suggested not a discipline plan but rather a philosophy to prepare children for a lifetime of responsible, appropriate behavior. Many have adapted his ideas to current day thought. Hey, whatever works! I'll help you weed through these endless ideas.

Your own understanding attitude is the number one thing that can really help your child. Self help experts, and more importantly other parents, agree that your child will benefit most from your own loving hand. So you need to make sure it's strong. Chapter Eight focuses on your job as parent and nurturer. A positive outcome is greatly up to you. All the helpful treatment, improved skills, etc. can't happen if you don't make it so. Tall order? You bet. In this chapter we take a look at how we parents personally deal with the job of fighting the ADD battle on behalf of our children. We'll check if we're being accountable to our children and to others needing our support. We'll take a look at advocacy and what it may mean for you. In addition, I provide an outline for your own plan of action that you can create, now that you know it's ADD.

As promised, Chapter Nine is devoted to your emotional and physical well being. Perhaps you've heard the saying, "You can't take care of anyone until you take care of yourself first." But it's so hard to do, I know! There's no time. It's too inconvenient. *Insert your excuse here.* Most of us know what we're supposed to do for ourselves, but we often need some motivation to do it. I've included quotes and quips chosen especially to help you reflect on yourself and your life. Learn to laugh at yourself, if you dare. It's really quite easy, we tend to do such hilarious things! If you can get away for a walk or a trip to the gym, that's great. If you can't, just flip through these pages for a mini get-away.

Finally you will find a resource section. It includes listings of associations, books and publications, on-line computer services, Internet addresses, and a glossary and index. These pages should help you to find the information you need in a hurry. Refer to it often.

2

WHAT IS ADD?

Prepare To Learn

Let's get started learning about ADD. Much effort has been made to present this information in a clear and helpful manner. I've tried to make it less intimidating and easier for you to convey to others. A solid knowledge of ADD is one of the most effective tools you can have as you interact with those who interact with your child, so here we go.

What Is ADD?

When someone remarks that your child is certainly a handful, or wonders aloud how you can possibly keep up with her, what's your reaction? You might say something like, "Yes, my Sara is a little hyperactive" or perhaps you launch into a textbook description of ADD, "A number of experts have hypothesized that a neurotransmitter deficiency in the brain causes many children to exhibit antisocial behavior." Huh? Well, maybe you wouldn't go that route. Maybe you go on the defense, "Well, at least he's not as bad as you-know-who" nodding in the direction of some kid acting worse than yours. Still, most of us simply cringe and zip our lips. We'd love to explain but ADD is just too complicated a topic.

And too, most people don't accept ADD as a legitimate reason behind what they believe to be unacceptable behavior. Most consider it an excuse. But, what we parents know is that there is something transforming our sweet, innocent children into uncontrollable, irresponsible, spaced-out strangers.

ADD is most often explained not as a specific disorder like diabetes or asthma for example, but as a group of characteristics and results. *Hyperactivity, distractibility, and weak impulse control are the main characteristics while the results are more varied - learning difficulties, sleeplessness, anxiety, poor social skills, etc.* Since many experts don't agree on its cause, that's what we have to work with. We parents know that a certain combination of behaviors and traits are showing up in our child again and again, causing him undo frustration and limiting his potential socially, academically and emotionally. This consistent presence of such behaviors and traits accompanied by some resulting difficulty is the scenario that moves our child from the playground onto the ADD battleground.

We can begin to diagnose ADD by watching how often such behaviors occur and the severity of their outcomes. How often does *what* occur? As noted before, the most typical characteristics that may be exhibited by a child affected by ADD include hyperactivity, distractibility and/or weak impulse control. Just what kind of behaviors constitutes one of these characteristics? And just how intense does the behavior have to be to label it as one of the three? Each characteristic is more fully described here.

Hyperactivity

In thinking back to my own school days I remember overhearing the second grade teachers discussing Eddie[2], the class clown. "He's not a bad boy, he's just so ... well, hyper." Eddie's hands and feet were constantly in motion. I know because he sat behind me and constantly kicked my chair and tugged on my pigtails. He also hummed to himself and made clicking noises with his tongue. Recess time was heaven for Eddie - he ran and climbed all over the playground, sometimes he would join us for a bit of dodge ball but he never stayed very long. Hyper, yes!

The term attention deficit disorder wasn't used so much in those 1960's, but even a seven-year-old knew what it meant to have "ants in the pants" like Eddie did. Hyperactivity is today described much as the behaviors shown by Eddie. *The hyperactive child exhibits an unusual amount of activity, although he doesn't usually run wild.* Something is always moving - feet, fingers, pencil. He squirms, fidgets or cannot stay seated.

Tammy, mother of nine-year-old Scott, agrees that hyperactivity isn't just limited to running wild. For Scott, sitting still is a real chore. Sitting with his feet on the floor and with good posture is almost impossible. If left alone at the kitchen table to tackle homework, Tammy may come back to find him in any of a number of postures - standing, with one knee on the chair, slouched half way down the chair with legs outstretched, sitting straight but with legs wrapped tightly around the chair, or sitting on the table with legs swinging away over a toppled chair. Scott also fidgets. He fidgets in the back seat of the car, he fidgets in the soft seat of a movie theater. "Scott is not very pleasant to sit next to on the couch," says

---

[2]Names have been changed throughout.

Tammy. "If he does finally get settled into a book or homework, he's humming, tapping fingers, pulling at his hair or singing. This drives Scott's father crazy. He can't understand why Scott always has to fidget. It can get to the point of screaming on my husband's part. Poor Scott doesn't realize he has been creating such a disturbance!"

Distractibility

When we think about the term attention deficit it is logical by definition to understand its meaning as a lack of attention. But there's more to it than just some missing factor. Our ADD child can pay attention overtime, actually. *The real meaning behind distractibility is in his inability to focus on the task at hand.* In the auditory (hearing) sense, the child pays attention to all sounds, not just those that are appropriate for the situation. In the visual (seeing) sense, he is aware of all things around him. So really, it's this keen sense of surroundings that translates into attention problems, not the lack of it. We all drift off at times, don't we? The trouble comes for our child who drifts away persistently and has a hard time drifting back. He can miss a lot. In addition, this habit of tuning into too much stimuli can overwhelm a child; the sights and sounds just won't rest. It's exhausting.

Mary's test results on her kindergarten entrance exam were excellent. A computerized rating scale noted average or above average skill in all areas except two - auditory perception and visual memory skills. In these areas Mary's results were rated as exceptionally above average. Mary's parents were quite satisfied, proud actually, that their daughter had such potential. They mused, maybe she'll be a musician with such keen sense of hearing, or perhaps some type of researcher with those wonderful memory skills. What a surprise when in first grade the teacher wrote home to Mary's parents in frustration.

Mary's dad shares a portion of the note with us: "Dear Mr. And Mrs. Smith, I'm having great difficulty with Mary in school. She is constantly daydreaming, looking out the window or staring into space. She doesn't complete her seat work, can't follow directions and has begun to distract other students." As you can imagine, this report was quite unexpected about their Mary. They thought perhaps she was bored, after all she had tested so well in the school entrance tests and her pre-school teachers always raved about her. No, boredom wasn't Mary's trouble. Mary's teacher noted that in many cases, when she saw an advanced student behaving as if bored, the student would at least have the required work completed before drifting or distracting others. A long search into the trouble behind Mary's distractibility (school counselor, psychologist, pediatrician, etc.) led them to the land of ADD.

Many times a child can make it through the school day, often shaking himself free of distractions and just barely staying on track. However, such a long battle with self-control tends to wear this child down, resulting in his letting loose once he gets home. Then, look out! Jeremy is such a child, as shared by his mother, Bev. Bev had accepted the fact that her son was a handful - he always had been full of energy. His grades in school were average, his teacher reporting that he was an energetic student and that she had come to count on him as her "backup brain" as she called him. Jeremy seemed to take note of the littlest things the teacher said, like the time she asked the class to remind her to pass out the book order forms at day's end. Only Jeremy remembered the request. If the teacher said that the class could do some extra activity if time permitted, Jeremy would note the fact and remind her.

Bev too, was mindful of his keen sense of awareness. As parents we have all responded to our kids' requests with a "We'll see, maybe later," secretly using the line hoping the request would be forgotten. Jeremy seldom forgot. But, the intensity of his ability to take it all in also became his challenge. Bev notes that after a day of taking in too much stimuli and struggling to stay in control, he tears into the house, uncontrollably rushing around, tense, and even defiant. Since he didn't show these behaviors during the school day, Bev just figured he was letting off steam and that she would just have to put up with it. The homework hour, though, was quite troublesome for the whole family. Since the quality of his homework was less than acceptable and because it was part of Jeremy's grades, Bev finally decided to begin the long journey toward a diagnosis of ADD, though like most of us she had no idea that was where the road would lead.

Distractibility is a normal behavior in children and adults of all ages. Remember last month at church service? You had been thinking about the vacation trip you had taken to the beach last August and just then, the collection basket was upon you! Yes, we all drift away, but most of us have some sort of filtering ability that allows us to focus only on the task or event at hand. We complete chores and assignments, and move on to the next thing with little frustration. A child without ADD working on multiplication tables, for example, can struggle through the page, yet still have some sense of completion. And while she may also storm into the house after a particularly rough day at school, it is not the everyday occurrence that plagues our ADD child and exhausts us. While distractibility is one of the main behavioral clues to ADD, it can be hidden as shared in the stories of Mary and Jeremy. Funny, in this world where most of us are trying to remind ourselves to stop and smell the roses and to brake for rainbows, our ADD kids already know how to do this with finesse. However, it is a delicate balance between following your instincts and performing as expected or required.

Impulsivity

In ADD circles, *impulsivity has become the buzz word to describe the behavior of acting on impulse or as having weak impulse control. The key to impulsive behavior as related to ADD is its persistence and resulting seriousness.* After all, we buy on impulse in the grocery checkout line, we smack at the mosquito on our neck on impulse, and emergency personnel make life saving decisions on impulse. However, for the child affected by ADD, impulsivity tends to be more the rule than the exception.

The child struggling with impulsivity as a result of ADD does not think before acting or talking. She doesn't consider the impact of her actions on others, thus, doesn't learn from experience or consequence. She can be accident prone. Parents report that their ADD children jump from high places like sliding boards and jungle gyms, leap out of tall trees, flip on and off the bed, and so on. They have the bruises to show for it all, too. A child's struggles with weak impulse control are frustrating for her and her caregiver.

Another example of weak impulse control comes from Michelle, an adorable four year old. Helpful and so smart, reported her baby-sitter. But, Michelle was the resident biter in this family day care home. Every child care center has one or two, biters that is. More than likely many of us reading this book are parents of biters, hopefully on the way to other, less physical acts when dealing with others. I'm not saying that biting is necessarily a clue to ADD. The clue is the impulsive nature of such an act. It's just that the result of a biting episode is, well... so evident. There it is - your child's dental imprint on the rosy soft skin of a playmate. As the bruise heals it begins to look even nastier. Michelle's father took blame at first, since he often played a little nibbling game with his daughter. He had read in a parenting magazine that for many biters, such play is normal. Perhaps, he had thought, she was just playing too. Then, another biting incident with yet another playmate showed cause for further alarm. It seemed Michelle was quite angry, almost wild during the confrontation and seemed to feel no remorse for her wrongdoing.

Certainly not all spats between children are impulsive in nature, and thankfully not all impulsive behavior ends with one child hurting another. Just as serious though, is when a child hurts himself because he doesn't think ahead to the consequences. "I was just so angry, and worried all at once", says Diane, mother of six-year-old Randy. Randy was always springing into action without hesitation. One day Randy was in the basement practicing karate moves on a kicking bag. Diane had just reached the bottom of the steps, in time to see Randy swinging upside down from the bag happily, until he let go... "He let out a huge scream and all I could think of was, broken neck" recalls Diane. Luckily there is some padding just under the kicking bag and Randy had rolled his head away from direct impact. It wasn't that he had accidentally fallen off the bag, he had just let go. On the one hand Diane was relieved that Randy was okay, yet steamed that he would even try such a stunt. "What came out of my mouth was, 'You should know better' when what I was feeling was 'Oh my God, he could've been really hurt', yet it's not an unusual episode around our house, " sighs Diane.

Besides the obvious potential of injury to your child or others, impulsivity can create some other really annoying habits. Anyone who interacts with an ADD child knows all too well that she will interrupt, talk out of turn or call out answers at any moment. Sandy, mother of nine year old Tina, says " I trained myself to make phone calls when Tina was outside or asleep, and let the answering machine pick up incoming calls. It seemed she couldn't let me talk on the phone for a minute at a time. Worse, she didn't seem to see how annoying her behavior was." Many parents deal with the old vying for attention routine. We learn to have a basket of toys nearby to direct a child toward, or we pause and say gently, "Now honey, it's not polite to interrupt." The ADD clue here is that our child just doesn't make that connection. She just doesn't see the impact of her actions on others. She may wonder why mom is so angry all of a sudden. She can't understand why the teacher is annoyed. After all she answered the question correctly didn't she?

Perhaps the thing that makes us craziest is that our child doesn't learn from experience. We struggle to create consequences to counter unwelcome behavior, just like the parenting manual instructed. But, the results are minimal at best. "You just never learn", you cry out before adding "Just what must I do to get you to stop doing these things?" The behavior-consequence connection is loose or non-existent for the ADD child. Karen shares this story about her seven-year-old nephew, Nathaniel. Nathaniel is a spiller. It seemed he spilled his drink at every meal. He would reach across the table, knocking over his glass. He would set his glass down too close to the edge of the table and knock it on to the floor. He would be enthusiastically telling about his day using full hand motions, when whoops, the drink was spilled again. His parents tried the logical consequences like having Nathaniel clean up his own messes, having him eat at a separate place from the table, and even not allowing him to enjoy a drink with dinner. But, and this brings us to another point about consequences, Nathaniel's behavior wasn't intentional; it was impulsive. And, it's hard to correct impulsive behavior with consequences alone. More about that in Chapter Seven.

What The Experts Say

The American Psychiatric Association (APA) notes that *"ADD is an enduring disorder that produces challenges in one's life."* Researchers suppose that while it most likely begins in infancy, it can extend throughout adulthood. ADD many times goes unnoticed until its effects cause problems in a child's life at home, school, or in a social environment. And, depending on a child's success at implementing social and behavioral skills, ADD may seem to "go away." It is conservatively estimated that between three and five percent of school aged children are affected by ADD. These children may have previously been labeled as learning disabled or socially immature. Only ten years ago these children were labeled as hyperactive, mentally challenged, etc., or were equated with emotionally disturbed or physically challenged children.

Attention disorders are the least common reason for hyperactivity, distractibility or impulsivity, according to the Learning Disabilities Association of America (LDAA). The most common cause for these behaviors are anxiety, depression, or physical illness. I recall when my Cassie first started having trouble in first grade. Her teacher hinted to me that something might be "wrong" at home. Abuse? Pending Divorce? Wimpy parenting style? While I certainly did not appreciate her judgment of our home life, she was indeed following the correct path by factoring out domestic and emotional problems as the root of a child's frustration and struggling in school.

What Exactly Are You Dealing With?

The APA suggests that there are three types of ADD. The first is known as *Attention Deficit/ Hyperactivity Disorder predominately hyperactive-impulsive type.* This type includes those who show significant problems with hyperactivity and impulsivity, but only some problem with inattention. The second, until a recent name change, was known as ADD without hyperactivity (ADD) or undifferentiated ADD. Today the term from the APA is *Attention Deficit Hyperactivity Order, inattentive type*. This group shows significant problems with inattention, but not much difficulty with impulsivity or hyperactivity. Finally, *Attention Deficit/Hyperactivity Disorder, combined type* includes those who show significant problems in all areas. Whew! No wonder it's so hard to get a solid diagnosis.

The Behavioral Survey
        The APA, as we found out previously, is the association that provides behavioral guidelines for diagnosing ADD. Those guidelines are listed in the *Diagnostic and Statistical Manual, 4th Edition (DSM IV-R)*. In order to diagnose a child as having *Attention Deficit/Hyperactivity Disorder predominately hyperactive-impulsive type*, the child must display at least six of the following characteristics for at least six months before the age of seven - along with a persistence of problems such characteristics may cause, in more than one setting, for example, home and school. Just think of it as how often, how long, and how serious.

Hyperactivity:
Fidgets, squirms or seems restless
Has difficulty remaining seated
Often runs about or climbs excessively in situations where it is
        inappropriate
Has difficulty playing quietly
Talks excessively
Is often "on the go" or acts as if "driven by a motor"

Impulsivity:
Difficulty awaiting turn
Blurts out answers
Interrupts or intrudes on others
Frequently engages in dangerous actions

The second form, *Attention Deficit/Hyperactivity Disorder, predominately inattentive type,* may be diagnosed if a child exhibits at least six of the following symptoms for a least six months, and to a greater degree than what is normally found in children of the same age. In addition the symptoms must have been apparent in the child before the age of seven and seriously impair a child's functioning in more than one setting, for example, home and school.

Distractibility
Fails to give close attention to details, makes careless mistakes
Difficulty sustaining attention
Does not seem to listen
Does not follow through on instructions, not due to not
    understanding instructions
Difficulty organizing tasks and activities
Reluctant to engage in tasks that require sustained mental effort
Often loses things necessary for tasks or activities
Easily distracted by extraneous stimuli
Forgetful in daily activities

Finally, to diagnose a child as having *Attention Deficit/Hyperactivity Disorder, combined type,* a child must exhibit at least a total of eight symptoms from the two lists for at least six months and before the age of seven, and those symptoms seriously impair a child's functioning in more than one setting, for example, home and school. Got that?

One reason for the requirement that the symptoms must have appeared before the age of seven is that certain learning disabilities left untreated can seem to produce behaviors similar to those of ADD. However, the effects stemming from learning disabilities will not usually surface until around age seven with the challenges of school work.

The APA reminds us not to use the lists as simple checklists or as the sole tool for diagnosis. The lists should be used with careful developmental history and observation to define a general pattern of behavior. Just how do we gather developmental history? In Chapter Three I offer instructions on starting a journal about your child. In this journal you will write about your child from infancy to now, considering her personality traits, dislikes, and the little things that bring her joy, among others. This process will help you recall and record observations that can help define developmental history and patterns of behavior. I remember how hard it was (still is) for my Cassie to settle down to sleep for a nap or for the night. Too much stimuli sent her into crying fits. Remember such things about your child; these observations are the developmental history the APA suggests we consider.

Tom, father of 11 year old Shawn, was so proud when his son began walking at ten months old. He recalls. "Oh, once I discovered he could walk, I encouraged Shawn to walk all the time. Actually it was more of a running-walk. Now, I think, gee whiz I should have kept him crawling a little longer cause I can't get him to slow down!" Observations like this will help you to make your diagnosis.

What Causes ADD?

Now that you're on your way to understanding ADD, you may be feeling some hope that you can finally help your child. Maybe you're also feeling somewhat angry that there exists such a disorder. Seems that something like this would have a solid treatment plan by now, or even better, a cure! Unfortunately, there is a wide disagreement over the origin of ADD and as a result, a wide array of possible treatment plans have emerged. Where does ADD come from? What causes it? How can I make sure any other kids I have won't "get it?" Here I offer various theories from past and present. We will look at their treatments in Chapter Four.

Why Now?

It is only within the last ten years that the term ADD has been widely used. Researchers trying to understand this disorder have found indications that ADD has been troubling people for centuries, labeled as minimal brain dysfunction, hyperkinetic reaction, hyperactivity, brain damage, etc. Medical professionals first noted the existence of ADD symptoms around 1900. If it has been plaguing us for so long, why wasn't it a problem *then?* Many changes in our society since the early 1900's have brought the effects of ADD's symptoms into the limelight.

Consider these possibilities. Changes like disappearing industrial jobs and their high wages have heightened the need for all students to stay and succeed in school. Advanced technology calls for, depends on, creative and flexible thinking; many times natural traits of our ADD kids (if properly channeled of course). The worth of such traits has been minimized in the past. On the educational front, many students with learning disabilities had been tucked away in special education classrooms. We have since demanded that schools accommodate all learners, providing appropriate education and remedial learning assistance. These days special needs students are often mainstreamed - receiving most of their education in regular classrooms with appropriate remedial support. Of course, this adjustment has not come easily, especially for teachers who face larger class sizes with less assistance. Finally, many laws drafted in the last twenty years for individuals with disabilities help to provide appropriate situations like opportunities for employment and equal access to services. Along with the opportunities came harsh penalties for discrimination involving these individuals. ADD has come along as one of these disabilities although still a widely disputed one. More on civil laws pertaining to ADD in Chapter Six.

Various Theories
　　　　The following are theories concerning the causes of ADD.

Early Theory and Diet Intervention
　　　　Back to our search for the cause of ADD. Turn of the century physicians believed that children who had incurred injuries to the head suffered brain damage, thus the reason for their difficult behavior. In more recent times some twenty years ago, allergist and pediatrician Dr. Benjamin Feingold discovered a relationship between behavioral patterns and a child's diet. He proposed that an adverse reaction to certain chemicals in foods, drinks, and medications was the cause of some children's hyperactive behavior. And, he found that when treating some children for allergies, their characteristic ADD traits diminished. Others adapted his initial assumptions to include preservatives and dyes found in the foods of that decade.
　　　　Among those foods, perhaps you remember one very notable scare which focused on the chemical coloring in red M&M's®. After twenty-seven years of including the red candies in the traditional M&M mix, the company removed it in 1976 because of what the company called misplaced concern over the food dye. The red M&M returned in the late eighties

and is now being joined by such colors as blue, plus a whole new color slate to be introduced in 1997, according to an article featured by the Associated Press (1996).

None the less, in the mid seventies Feingold's claims began to include the notion that adverse reactions to these substances were responsible for a variety of children's learning, behavior, and attention challenges. However, he found that only 2 to 4 percent of ADD children responded to the treatment called for in his theory. Those results, added to the sheer inconvenience of sticking to a limited diet helped the theory fade away as a cause of ADD.

Feingold's work lives on though as new proponents of the original theory strive to help those they can. Dr. Doris Rapp, author of *Is This Your Child? Discovering & Treating Unrecognized Allergies* (William Morrow, 1991) believes that allergic reactions to a host of things are indeed the root of learning and behavioral disorders. Her work has created a whole new group of Feingold followers who believe dietary and environmental intervention is the cure for the cause.

Chemical Imbalance

The prevailing theory from the medical and psychological profession, as reported in a fact sheet published by the national group Children and Adults with ADD (CHADD), is that ADD is caused by a chemical imbalance in the brain. In 1990, *The New England Journal of Medicine* reported that researchers at the National Institute for Mental Health used advanced brain imaging techniques to look at the metabolism of "normal" adults as compared to the metabolism in adults affected by ADD. Metabolism shows the rate at which the brain uses glucose - the brain's primary energy source. The researchers found that the ADD adults used this energy source at a lower rate than those without ADD. Further, they found this lower metabolism rate to be most evident in the part of the brain most important for attention, handwriting, motor control and self-control. Whew! What you have just learned is that the field of medicine now considers ADD to be a neurobiological disorder, meaning that it is related to the brain and body. So, does it mean that now we parents can rejoice? "Oh thank goodness, it's not our fault", we cheer. On the other hand, maybe we curse our spouse's side of the family for passing on the genes for a bad brain! David Wodrich, Ph.D. reported in his book, *What Every Parent Wants to Know* (Brookes Publishing Co. 1994) that experts who have examined all of the current inheritance studies have concluded, "research shows that ADD can be understood as between 30% to 50% inherited..." So, experts do consider family history when considering low brain metabolism as the cause of ADD. Still feeling guilty? Me too.

This neurobiological theory provides testimony for the widespread use of stimulant medications in the treatment of ADD. These medications are thought to energize the brain's metabolism rate, helping it to use glucose at a more effective rate. In turn, this chemical messenger sends a wake up call to that area of the brain responsible for sustained attention and self-control, key components lacking in those affected by ADD. The term neurotransmitter, used in many ADD texts, is a naturally occurring chemical messenger. The term chemical imbalance, then refers to the deficiencies of these messengers. This theory is the most widely accepted today, along with its primary treatment, medication. However, many parents are uncomfortable about the possible side effects and negative connotations of dispensing daily doses of any medication. I explore the pros and cons of medication in Chapter Four. In any case, the search for cause and effect continues. Read on.

Inner Ear Imbalance

Harold N. Levinson, MD has provided much personal insight gathered from years of diagnosing and treating ADD and learning disabled patients. His popular books, namely *Total Concentration* (M Evans & Co., 1990) note the theory that an imbalance in the inner ear is culprit to many learning disabilities and ADD. More specifically, he focuses on the cerebral vestibular system (CVS). The cerebellum is part of the brain that controls coordination of voluntary movement. The vestibular system includes receivers found in the inner ear that respond to gravity and position and movement of the head. Together this CVS system regulates energy levels, balance, speech and language, memory, moods and so on. Levinson cites that problems arise when an imbalance, whether naturally occurring or caused by illness, infection or injury, occurs in the CVS system, thus creating the characteristics of ADD and learning problems.

He insists that the proper regimen of medications, whether stimulants, antihistamines, anti-motion sickness meds, etc., can over time correct the effects of ADD as the patient also learns self monitoring techniques. Those techniques include things like checking in with oneself and asking "Am I on task? Am I paying attention?" The key to effective treatment according to Levinson is to determine the correct type and dosage of medications. The hope of short term (in comparison to life-time) medical treatment appeals to many parents. And, it does put faith in a child's abilities to help herself.

Colored Lenses

The theory of colored lenses providing relief for some effects of ADD, like inability to sustain focus, was introduced in the late 1980's by Helen Irlen, a California psychologist. She believes that learning disabilities and attention deficits are caused by a neurological condition called Scotopic Sensitivity Syndrome (SSS). In her book, *Reading by the Colors* (Avery Publishing Group, 1991), Irlen describes SSS as a condition causing perceptual problems. Problems occur through the manner we visually perceive light wavelength and color contrast. That perception, she says, is bothersome for those with this condition.

Irlen speculates that a child with SSS uses more energy for reading and other visual activities and thus becomes fatigued, distracted and unable to maintain focus. Further, she suggests that almost 50% of reading disabled individuals suffer from SSS. The main component of treatment involves fitting the individual with glasses having specially tinted lenses called Irlen lenses or Irlen filters. Other treatment components are choosing appropriate task lighting and using colors that do not offend the vision. The tinted lenses (and to a lesser degree the color and light choices) tend to lessen the discomfort caused by SSS, thus easing some learning difficulties and having a positive impact on ADD characteristics as well.

Personality Differences

There are some in the professional fields who suggest yet another reason for the evidence of ADD; personality differences. Thom Hartmann, an entrepreneur, director of a residential treatment facility, and author of *ADD - A Different Perspective* (Underwood-Miller, 1993) suggests that the ADD personality is parallel to that of a hunter; constantly monitoring, quickly acting, always looking for that instant reward. The non - ADD personality, then, is described as a farmer; going by the rules, planting and waiting for the harvest, knowing that in time his rewards will come.

Hartmann, a self-described "hunter," provides great insight into the characteristics of the ADD person using the hunter metaphor, as compared to the opposite farmer. I enjoyed this book. It helped me to notice my kids strengths and talents that are many times masked by ADD's bothersome effects. Theories such as Hartmann's point to a lack of understanding of personality types on the part of others as a reason for the unacceptable actions of the ADD labeled person. Problem is, we are faced with either persuading a society with set opinions and bias to accept our child's personality differences, or helping our child adapt enough to survive and thrive in that society.

Hartmann notes that his theory is not designed to replace traditional treatment methods, but to promote an understanding that there is nothing "wrong" or "bad" about ADD, just different.

Symmetric Tonic Reflex

Another theory about the cause of ADD comes from over 25 years of research at the University of Indiana. There, Dr. Nancy O' Dell and Dr. Mary Cook recognize a physical and curable cause of ADD. The theory stems from research in the field of reflexology. Apparently, most of us develop and then lose a certain reflex through the act of crawling. This reflex, the symmetric tonic reflex, helps us in our development. However, if it does not diminish over time, as other reflexes in infancy do (for example the sucking reflex), it is said to cause much discomfort for the ADD person. Why would it not diminish? Not enough time spent crawling say Drs. O' Dell and Cook in their upcoming book (Avery Publishing Group). A child who walked early or spent a lot of time in a walker may be at risk. The non - ADD person cannot possibly experience the particular discomfort this leftover reflex causes. The resulting consequences of this discomfort then are the traits that show up as ADD.

Special exercises to diminish this leftover reflex have proven to reduce and even cure ADD effects in many instances. Not to be confused with chiropractic treatment, meaning physical manipulation of the bones and muscles, this therapy focuses on working the body *through* the reflex, just as it should have occurred naturally as part of a child's development. See the Resource Section for the address where you can reach Drs. Cook & O'Dell. Don't look for a discussion of this theory in the standard ADD texts. Most books on ADD, as you may already have found, won't discuss those theories that have not yet provided an undeniable seal of proof. I discuss the details of this, and other treatments in the next chapter.

What Else?

Fortunately, these aren't the last words on ADD. Research and theorizing continue. As parents we must insist that they do. What if there's something out there that relieves our child of the frustration of ADD forever, without having to struggle with behavior modification plans or drugs? If there is such a something I want to know about it, and so do you. Till then, keep an open mind and consider facets of all theories. There could be some component of its treatment that really helps your child. Next, we start our detective work.

Your Child Needs A Champion

3

HOW WE FIND OUT ABOUT ADD, HOW WE DON'T, WHY WE MUST

Now That You Know ADD

Now that you know more about ADD, what it is and what it isn't, prepare to become an ADD - Detective. In this chapter you'll learn how to search for and recognize the clues that can begin to solve the case for your child.

When It's Not Cute Anymore

Remember when your relatives delighted in the antics of your toddler? Uncle Harry used to encourage Junior to jump into his waiting arms for a flight around the living room on broad shoulders. Grandpa would cheer as your daughter rolled across the floor like a log heading for the paper mill. He even made it competitive by timing the event. Oh, but those days are long gone. Such behavior isn't cute anymore. Relatives tell you what a "handful" your child has become and let you know in no uncertain terms that if the kid were theirs, such behavior would *not* be permitted. And it's just not your relatives. The grocery store manager used to blow raspberries at your sweet cherub, and rewarded her with crackers for sitting so nicely in the cart - she was strapped in, where could she go? These days Mr. Manager has a quite different look on his face. Hands on hips, glare in his eyes, he stands guard at the end of the cereal aisle, sizing up your little shopper. No reward today, only a very loud list of what she'd better not do in his store.

So you tell yourself that maybe it is time for your child to grow out of such wild behavior. You guess you need to expect a higher level of obedience from your child, a certain manner of excellent behavior. Quite a tall order for a five year old though, to be molded into the model of the perfectly behaved, perfectly parented young child. Hey, but look around! Other children seem to be doing it okay, why can't yours? You ask yourself if your parenting style is really *that* bad. Maybe you begin to hide from certain situations. You begin to rotate shopping among three or four different grocery stores. Family dinner out? It's not worth the extra effort so you just eat in. Date with your spouse? Hah! You've worn out all the dependable baby sitters months ago. Home is your safe haven, your societal hideout.

Venturing Out In The World

Soon a time comes when you can no longer hide out, no longer want to take a back seat to life. For the sake of your child you stop hiding. It is your child's time for friends, school and activities. And, it's your responsibility to guide her, encourage him, fostering confidence and self esteem. You've been coping okay in the solitude of your home, but now comes the time to join the rest of the world, whether the world approves or not.

Maybe you have been stronger than many of us. You may have ignored the judgments of others and lived each day with your "handful" as if the rest of the world was just too particular. Good for you! I envy your strength and spirit. But alas, the time comes when that all-important good attitude is not enough. Maybe it's the day your child meets the structure of school and his success is hampered by his spirited personality. You know his potential, you are quite aware of his strengths - school should be a pleasure but it becomes a hardship. Maybe that innovative pre-school your daughter attended was an exception. The teachers there praised her achievements, said she was very advanced. Yet her kindergarten performance is anything but advanced. In fact you've been told that your daughter is disruptive and whiny. Where did such behavior suddenly come from? It is the school or is it the child?

Something or someone brought you to this point, whether it was your own intuition hinting that something just wasn't right, negative reports sent home from your child's teacher, or seeing your child's own frustration. What and where exactly is this point you've reached? Welcome to the edge of what you'll come to know as the awareness cycle. Come on, jump in! Levels in the cycle include: ignorance (an unawareness of ADD), denial (a rejection of the existence of ADD or its affects), exploration (a search to learn about ADD and it's relationship to your child), and acceptance (an attitude that helps to formulate a plan of action, it is not a state of giving up or giving in.)

These levels help us to move through a cycle of awareness where we can ultimately choose the actions that will be most effective. There are a number of psychological models that the profession utilizes to explain the processes we experience when facing a challenge or change in our lives. I learned about these processes in a former life as a professional trainer and saw a similarity between the processes and those levels of awareness we parents encounter, knowingly or not, as we attempt to deal with the effects ADD has on our children. The awareness cycle addresses the focus of this chapter - How We Find Out About ADD, How We Don't, Why We Must.

Knowing About The Levels Of Awareness Can Help

The awareness levels that we encounter on our journey are labeled as Ignorance, Denial, Exploration, and Acceptance. The idea is that whenever we face a challenge or change in our lives we experience each level at least once before we make the change or act to face the challenge. We may become stalled at a certain level, choosing to ignore such change especially if it is thrust upon us in a negative manner. Depending on to what degree a challenge takes us by surprise, we may visit certain levels for only a short or a seemingly long while. We might move around the cycle a lot, visiting between exploration and denial for example, each time we read a new perspective or learn some new information. We may feel as if we're getting no where fast when it all gets too overwhelming. Because our own feelings are connected to the levels of awareness, we begin our ride on the emotional roller coaster. Most of us hold season passes to that attraction. Don't be concerned how much time or effort you're spending in each level because each person has their own way of reacting in each level. Do be concerned if you just can't seem to see beyond today. This can be a sign of being stuck for too long in one place. Don't be alarmed, this discussion is not designed to be a psychotherapy exercise. By knowing what levels are involved in the awareness cycle you can review where you are now and take action to discover if ADD is the suspect of your child's frustration. If you already know that it is ADD, your attention to what happens in each level will help you continue your ongoing plan of action that will help your child.

Ignorance

No, this doesn't mean *you* are ignorant. It refers to ADD ignorance, not knowing that such a thing exists, what it is, or what effects it causes. Most of us begin our journey out of ADD ignorance. After all, isn't ADD the label attached to those kids whose parents can't handle them or who don't want to be bothered to try? That's what Emily used to believe. That was before her daughter came home from school with an unexpected mid-marking period report, one filled with much criticism. It seemed that Tracy's behavior was getting to be more than her teacher could handle. Six-year-old Tracy was bright and creative, but she could not follow directions, annoyed other children, would not sit still or wait her turn in the lunch or recess lines. Time outs (isolated, quiet time away from the group) were not effective as Tracy continually talked out of turn and ignored her seat work, reported the teacher. This report was quite unsettling for Emily, who supervised Tracy's homework each evening and paid close attention to papers and test scores that were brought home, even in a very messy backpack. Tracy could be stubborn, especially at homework time, became excited easily, and rarely sat still. Yet, the unsatisfactory report was hard to accept. So Emily began as most of us would, by blaming herself then taking it upon herself to try harder. What did she try harder to do? Well she scolded herself for being too lenient in her parenting responsibilities, for working outside the home too long and too hard, and for using only her gut instinct where Tracy's discipline was concerned. Emily attended a parenting workshop where she learned how to use consequences, reward charts, and an un-emotional tone of voice, all which the workshop leader guaranteed would work if used consistently. She tried all these tactics. She tried them and she tried them and she tried them. Sometimes these tactics seemed to be effective, but then again, sometimes Tracy seemed oblivious to her mother's efforts. The tactics didn't seem to stick. The ADD ignorance factor came into play because although Emily was trying really hard, normal parenting skills don't always work for ADD kids. If Emily knew that ADD was a concern, she could have adjusted her use of the tactics she had learned.

Seeing little improvement, Tracy's teacher suggested that there might be some undo anxiety at home causing her disruptive behavior; parental arguing, alcoholism, abuse? Angry at the teacher's judgment but willing to try anything for Tracy's sake, Emily began trying to "fix" herself. While the teacher was on the right track - most hyperactive and inattentive behavior is not a result of ADD but of anxiety, emotional trouble, or illness - her questioning sent Emily into a self help whirlwind. She tried counseling where she learned she might be too controlling. She read books that pointed to her emotional attitude as a key problem. She wrote in her journal about her childhood; hey, maybe it wasn't as functional as she had remembered. After this self improvement stint the household seemed less hectic, a rigid schedule loosened, but Emily quite frankly wasn't convinced that any of it helped at all. By the third marking period Emily was hanging in there but making little improvement. Tracy's teacher continued an array of criticism, writing "sloppy" and "careless" in big red letters on most of Tracy's work. Emily just hoped that Tracy could make it through to the end of the school year without a major incident. Even though Emily had tried to move out of the ignorance level by "accepting" she was at fault, and by "exploring" different ways to improve her parenting skills, she was stuck in ignorance because she didn't know about ADD and its effects. Her efforts had minimal effects in comparison.

Incidentally, it wasn't until mid way through Tracy's second year that the family finally learned about ADD. With a new and positive teacher, Tracy seemed to respond nicely to second grade and the cheerful "Keep Trying" and "You're getting there" remarks on her papers. Emily figured that the first grade teacher must have been exaggerating. It seemed there was nothing to worry about for now. However, that was just a different level of awareness Emily had reached - Denial.

Denial

ADD Denial can appear in many ways and at a variety of times. A parent may absolutely believe that there is no concern for intervention, even when the teacher's note comes home. For the child who isn't too much of a behavior problem, is an average student, yet faces frustration in school, a typical response from mom or dad may be that there's nothing wrong with the child so it must be the school or the teacher's methods. Jeff, parent of seven-year-old Nick, recalls his time in the denial level. "My own father, a retired business person, kept telling me not to worry about Nick's problems in school. Nick is an average student and sometimes he disrupts the other kids when he is supposed to be working independently. So, my father would say that the whole school system was lacking, trying to find labels for kids and excuses to give for not turning out capable students. His advice was to ignore the teacher's notes. 'Nick is probably just bored', he'd say." But, Nick's problems persisted as he fell further and further behind in his studies while daydreaming the school hours away.

Some may believe the best thing is to let sleeping dogs lie, as the saying goes. The situation isn't really that traumatic so we choose not to act, hoping that whatever is wrong will go away. Or, we remain silent figuring that our intervention might just make things worse. That was the case with George, who saw too many other parents making a huge commotion over their kids. It seemed to him that some parents would be knocking down the principal's door every time their kid complained about something or someone. Not him. So, when George Jr. brought home a detention notice for homework not turned in. he did nothing. Although he knew George Jr. had completed the work (he had personally signed each assignment) George believed that his son needed to take responsibility to work things out for himself. George was not about to become one of those whining adults who embarrassed their kids at school. But, taking responsibility for oneself is not always easy, especially with ADD thrown in.

We can face denial many times throughout the course of our challenge with ADD. Even though we may have researched the topic to great length (exploration), have instituted helping measures at home and at school, we may drift back to denial at almost any time. Sherri is an eight-year-old who loves animals, after school soccer, and fighting with her six year old brother. Her parents, Jean and Bill, have been following a plan of action that includes helping Sherri to improve organization skills for school work and studying, and using positive reinforcement to foster good behavior. Things seem to go well for a few weeks at a time. This plan of action takes effort on everyone's part and sometimes Sherri just doesn't produce results like "she should." Her grades may slip, she is mean to the dog or her brother, and her soccer coach has to give her yet another time out. Then her parents lament, "It doesn't matter what we try, no matter what we do, nothing helps. We just don't know what to do with ourselves anymore." It's so easy to feel failure when such an important person, your child, is suffering. Even though you suspect it's ADD and even though you realize that it's an extremely frustrating challenge, it is still a lot easier to blame yourself, just as Jean and Bob did. Such a feeling of helplessness whirls us right back to that level of denial, leaving us to ask ourselves where we fell short, looking for some other reason for our troubles.

We may fall into a bit different type of denial, that of being a victim and trying to find every instance where we can shift the blame elsewhere. Maybe it was some weird genetic thing passed on by Great Grandpa Jeremiah on your husband's side of the family. Perhaps you blame your wife, after all she never limits the kids' sugar consumption and she lets them get away with murder! The fault could lie with your child's reaction to pollutants in the environment. But did you get around to putting in that water filtration system or air cleaner? Maybe it's society at fault. I visited denial several times arguing that point to myself. I declared that my two kids' only real trouble was that no one else but me understood their unique and carefree personalities. I felt like no one else cared enough to try a little harder to find a way to get through to them.

There are many reasons to deny that a child has a disorder such as ADD. These reasons may secretly give us hope that it just ain't so. We hope that it'll go away. We hope that others won't notice and that it won't harm our child very much. But in denial we run the risk of ignoring some real troubles that ADD brings with it. That is the danger.

Exploration

At this point in time, you are already exploring. I know, because you have chosen to read this book. That's a great start, and when you're through with it I hope you'll continue to explore other titles focusing on learning disabilities, emotional health, etc. This level of awareness helps you to focus your energy on the particular challenge, instead of on yourself or the job you've done as a parent. Exploration helps you to move away from blaming yourself or others for your child's frustration. It helps you to move toward action to help your child. In exploring, you're searching for clues, bits and pieces of information that will help you to accept this challenge and finally to do something about it.

On Your Own

Some of us begin to explore independently while some of us explore with the help of others. Debra recalls how her determination to help her child led to her exploration of ADD. She says, "I just knew there had to be something else that would help my son, Chad. We had reduced TV time and every night I worked side by side with him on homework assignments. Yet, his teacher still noted that it was hard to keep Chad focused, especially when students were expected to work alone like on math sheets or during silent reading time. I knew he was struggling in school because his behavior at home was beginning to worsen. I couldn't get him to sit for more than five minutes at a time. As is my style, I spent an afternoon in the library pouring through the child development section. The librarian showed me how to use the electronic card catalog to narrow the subjects I was searching for. She showed me how to enter words together such as child + stress + learning. It worked! This search led me to a section of books that were not in the parenting section of the library. I found a whole row of books covering physical and mental developmental issues related to children. Still it took some time to piece together the symptoms the teacher and I had observed in Chad and to link those with any of a number of causes. And, it was a monumental task to weed out what I thought was unrelated and what might be helpful. All my efforts did eventually lead me on a path toward a diagnosis. Then I felt confident that I could do some good for Chad."

Debra's exploration, almost detective like in her manner, unfortunately is the way a lot of us learn about ADD. Just peek inside the margins of library books on this subject. You'll see passages underlined, starred or even highlighted, the evidence that others are exploring, too. My own first search in my city's public library led me to a book that pointed to abnormalities of the inner ear as the root cause of learning and attention problems. Thinking that the author was referring to the middle ear and since neither of my kids had more than one or two prescriptions of the pink stuff (amoxycillin) during their young lives, I cast the information off. I did eventually wander back to that book, *Total Concentration* by Harold N. Levinson, M.D. -referenced in Chapter Two. The inner ear imbalance may be the right connection for some, but I chose to ignore it initially. So while exploring on your own is an excellent way to begin, just know that it's real easy to miss or misunderstand some piece of information that can truly help.

Others Who Can Help You To Explore
The Pediatrician

Begin with a visit to your child's pediatrician. Physical illness like a lingering flu virus or the early stages of an overactive thyroid, for example, can sometimes cause symptoms that are similar to those caused by ADD;   irritability, inattentiveness, trouble sitting still, etc. In addition to ruling out and/or clearing up any illnesses your child may be fighting, your pediatrician can detect a visual or hearing impairment and prescribe a visit to a specialist in that area. Your child's pediatrician can refer you to other professionals in her network that may provide counseling, support, or learning opportunities.

Teachers

While the support of your child's teacher is essential, he may also be an excellent source to help you with exploration. Most teachers will be glad to let you know where you can find further information on ADD, learning disabilities, behavior modification , etc. Their role in teaching should include helping you to formulate a plan to follow for school and at home, especially if something is hampering a child's success.   Formally called an *Individualized Education Plan (IEP)* when required by educational policy, such a plan addresses not only academic but behavioral issues as well. Even if a student has not been formally granted an IEP through diagnosis of learning disabilities, a helpful teacher can help you craft a plan for your child.

Now, we all know some caring teachers who do their duties quite well, and we all know some in the educational system who find it easier to let someone (you) or something else (detention) deal with a "problem child." Even worse may be the educator who allows a student to slip through her grade without alerting parents about problems the child has been facing. Oh, and this does happen. Many parents have shared such stories. Here is just one:

Linda's third grade report card didn't begin to hint at academic problems, much less ADD. B's and C's seemed to be the usual outcome, not too bad for a rigid private school, so thought Linda's family. Since her parents both worked full time, Linda spent afternoons at an after school care center where the caregivers provided a balanced schedule including snacks, physical activity and study time. Two of Linda's classmates also attended the center, so they usually worked on homework together, sometimes enlisting the help of an older student or adult. This arrangement seemed to be working well for Linda and her parents were satisfied that her efforts in school were on track. They were also pleased that the after school program provided activities to keep their energetic daughter occupied. The family arrived home week nights around 6:30 PM in time to have supper, see that homework was completed (they had been instructed not to correct the work), then rush to meetings, swim classes, or whatever else was on the schedule. Back home around 8 or 9 PM, there was sometimes a little time for TV, then off to bed. While this may sound like a typical 1990's family, Linda's active schedule and homework structure coupled with no negative reports from teacher formed the perfect screen to hide her academic problems.

What problems? None were evident until Linda's year in fourth grade. Parents of fourth graders know that grade four is a transition year at most schools. Linda's school was no exception - fourth grade was deemed one of the toughest because of the increasing need for students to think independently. Not only did fourth graders change classrooms three times per day, three different teachers each gave their own assignments. Students were expected to be well organized, to copy assignments from the board within a specified time, and to maintain an increasingly longer span of attention, among other things. Oh, and only one recess period! Parents were told, in a letter from the fourth grade teachers, to just be patient for the first month of school if their child seemed frustrated with the new schedule. But, by the second month Linda just couldn't cope with it all. Her ability to maintain focus now seriously undeveloped, she misunderstood her teachers' instructions and rarely finished copying all the notes from the board. She didn't ever seem to have the right books or supplies when she needed them. She had squeaked by other years only with the help of her classmates and by fooling (so she thought) her teachers. Now, everything was messed up. School was getting to be a blur. She began to complain of stomach and head aches, begging to stay home from school day after day. A physical exam didn't show any illness, so back to school Linda went. She began to visit the school nurse quite frequently, often going three times per day - once during each class switch. It was through the nurse, finally, that Linda's parents were alerted to her problems.

When Linda's parents met with her homeroom teacher and the school principal, they were surprised when the principal read to them from a folder describing Linda's progress over the last several years at the school. While kindergarten through second grades seemed to be somewhat challenging for Linda, remarks sighted her young developmental age as a factor. Linda was 5 years to the day when she started kindergarten, and teachers had assured her parents that she'd catch on sooner or later. However, it was a real blow to discover the observations most likely provided by the third grade teacher - yet none of which had been shared with them before. It was as if the folder held things intended only for other teachers' eyes. " It was written as kind of a warning label - teach at your own risk" says Linda's Dad. Remarks included such things as "doesn't pay attention", "can't follow directions", and "disturbs other students when she is supposed to be working independently."

Linda's parents wondered how such problems could have been overlooked? How could Linda have earned B's, even C's? The school psychologist suggested that Linda most likely adapted to the rigid structure of school and day care, and *that* combined with the family's busy lifestyle and her parents' patient and understanding natures masked her problems. Masked? No, not masked - here were teachers sharing critical knowledge about a child that could affect her academic success and self esteem indefinitely! But, without Linda's own attempt at relieving her frustration by missing classes and without the intervention of a caring school nurse, her ADD and resulting problems may have been minimized for years.

If you think this type of thing is rare, think again. If you assume that most teachers are caring and passionate about all students, listen closely at the next school open house. I find out most about what's going on at my kids' school by nosing in on other parents' conversations as they stand around outside the school waiting to pick up their kids. More on working with teachers in Chapter Six.

Learning Specialists

Others in school who can help you explore the topic of ADD are learning specialists, sometimes called remedial specialists. These helpers are trained to measure academic skill level and to teach those skills in a variety of ways. Unlike a tutor, who may be enlisted to help a child practice and review such skills, a learning specialist finds and uses alternate methods of teaching that can help a child to learn when traditional methods aren't effective. The school usually requires written permission from you if your child needs to meet with a learning specialist. Why? One reason is that funding may be provided by state or federal programs through an intermediate educational unit (IU). These specialists are usually employed by the IU and not directly by your child's school. Teachers may send your child to a tutor during school hours for extra practice on some skill. While most teachers will inform you when a child requires this extra help, written parent permission is not usually sought. Even if your child is not currently enrolled in a remedial program, you should certainly call upon these specialists for information regarding ADD and other learning topics. Most will be glad to hear from you. As one learning specialist at my kids' school said to me, "Mrs. Miller, you're doing so much good to just care enough to ask." Thanks, I needed that.

School Psychologists

Just what is a school psychologist? *A psychologist is trained to study human behavior and sometimes specializes in the intellectual, emotional, or educational fields.* The school psychologist has earned a Doctorate of Philosophy (Ph.D.) degree with special emphasis in education and also has acquired a license to practice in a particular state. In contrast, *a psychiatrist also specializes in human behavior, but in addition has earned a medical degree and is able to prescribe certain medications.* The school psychologist might conduct programs such as drug and alcohol awareness and keeps an open door for children with non-traditional families or those with emotional problems. If your school offers a coping program of any type, best bet is that the school psychologist is its facilitator. This professional can also help you and your child to adjust to challenges presented by ADD. Turn to this behavioral specialist for advice in setting up a system of positive reinforcement or other tactics that can ease the frenzy in your child's life. School psychologists are typically available only on a limited basis due to budget restraints. Many are shared by an entire school district consisting of a number of school buildings. So, it may take some extra effort to enlist the services of this helper. I have found that these professionals can get their hands on a whole host of videos, books, etc. Try sending a note if your calls are not returned. It is perfectly okay for you to call out of the blue - a recent brochure sent home from my kids' school noted that anyone can refer themselves or others to the school psychologist. There are times when you need to go by the chain of command (for testing for example), but not in your quest for information.

School Counselors

Your school may have a school counselor, who may or may not be a licensed psychologist. A counselor without such credentials may provide similar services but may not have the unique training in the learning processes to effectively identify and treat disorders affecting learning. The school counselor typically focuses on career and curriculum guidance for middle and high school students, but sometimes she may be called upon to handle those issues of mental or emotional health that affect a child. While these issues should be reserved for the psychologist, sometimes the listening ear of a caring counselor can ease a child's concerns. The counselor often works with those details relating to a student's goals and aspirations, so he is an excellent source to help you uncover your child's special talents and strengths. When things like hyperactivity or lack of focus shroud your child's special gifts, the career counselor can suggest or administer a variety of aptitude tests that can, in general, indicate a child's areas of excellence.

Other School Helpers

Although many of the assistants (some are paid, some are not) that help out in your child's classroom are there without any advanced training or education (some have both), these helpers can provide insight about your child that you or the teacher may have overlooked. Six-year-old Gregory had been struggling during group reading time. His teacher reported that he could not sit still, made annoying noises, and thus disrupted the rest of the class. It was Myra, a teacher's helper, who noticed that Gregory didn't exhibit the same behavior during the time he spent at an independent listening area. The listening area was tucked into a corner of the room where the children could stretch out at will and listen to taped stories through a pair of headphones. Myra noticed that Gregory did indeed stretch out, slouching low in his chair with legs outstretched, head cocked to one side against the chair back. It looked fairly uncomfortable to Myra, but Gregory could sit still in this way through an entire tape, seemingly absorbed. Comprehension checks proved that he indeed was listening to the story. In comparison, group reading time took place on a carpet on the floor, where the children were expected to sit cross legged or with knees bent, fairly close together. His teacher allowed him to enjoy the taped stories instead, just glad that there was some activity that kept Gregory settled. She was careful to explain this exception to the other children; they seemed to be glad that he could stay quiet for a change. But, she had not made the 'physical connection' until Myra mentioned it. Now Gregory is allowed to sit a bit away from the reading group where he can stretch out and enjoy a little personal space, thanks to Myra. Gregory's parents could not have noticed such a difference at home.

Every bit of information you can gather might help you piece together this puzzle you're working on. A classroom assistant helped me to discover that my Joey's defiant and angry behavior at home was not mirrored in school. Our kids played soccer together, so I would get these casual reports that Joey was very sweet and cooperative, yet that he was very frustrated with his work. That helped me focus on what I could do to ease his school day, instead of beefing up the discipline plan at home!

Community

Any of the mentioned helpers may be able to clue you in on meetings and seminars in the community that may help. Or, call the mental health association or counseling center in your town. They can tell you what your community has to offer as related to ADD or other child related topics. Our local YMCA featured such a presentation as part of its child care program. You may find that your city is one of many that sponsors a local chapter of the national group Children and Adults with Attention Deficit

Disorders (CHADD). This group typically offers monthly meetings designed to encourage parent to parent support as well as to provide education. CHADD's national chapter provides a newsletter, fact sheets, and a bi-monthly magazine to those who pay an annual fee. Most local CHADD meetings are held free of charge. Information on CHADD is listed in the Resource Section of this book. If there is a teaching hospital in your locale call the information desk and ask about services such as parent information centers, referral service phone lines or ADD divisions. Many times these hospitals' programs are funded by federal grants which tie into programs for families with special needs like us. Or, call the governor's hotline in your state. Most states have a special phone number listed in the government services pages of the phone book.

Cyberspace

One other resource that I have found is in Cyberspace, on the Internet. "Cyberspace" and "on-line" are just fancy names for "out there in computer land." If you have access to a computer with a modem (it connects your computer to other computers using the phone line) you can talk electronically to others from around the world on most any subject. Most commercial on-line services like CompuServe, America On-Line, and The Microsoft Network offer "chat sessions." The commercial services guide you to chat sessions with the click of a mouse or by having you type in a certain keyword. For example, you can connect with people who are also facing ADD challenges to exchange ideas, give support, or let off steam. One caution; these are not trained professionals in most cases, but are parents and others facing the same types of ADD challenges you and I face everyday. It doesn't hurt to have that extra ear available. And, many are interactive which means you can type in a question and someone will answer almost instantly. Some services provide special ADD related presentations on-line featuring psychologists, authors, and other professionals. You can ask questions through a mediator, although a responses may come slowly, or not at all. I have listed some of the commercial providers in the Resource Section. Do be aware of sales oriented information on the Internet. There are some fantastic resources that you can purchase on-line, but there are some questionable services as well. One resource I found offered "on-line ADD evaluations and recommendations," for $225.00. I don't think your insurance company would be too prompt in reimbursing that claim.

Ask, And Ask Again:
So you're learning all you can about this thing that is troubling your child. You may now feel a bit more armed to discuss your child's problems with others. If you suspect that ADD is the thing that's troubling your child, you need to discover to what extent. It's time to go beyond the general exploration stage. You'll now need to ask more questions that can be answered only by others who interact with your child. Who to ask? What to ask? Ask teachers, care givers, coaches, and the other helpers who know your child. The types of questions you ask will vary depending on your particular child's challenges, but the questions will focus on the effects, the behaviors exhibited by your child, and suggested solutions. If it's attending to seat work at school that is troublesome, ask the teacher what behaviors are evident and how he thinks the situation can be improved. Behavior problems at soccer practice? Ask the coach why she thinks it's occurring and ask her to suggest a way to curb the behavior. If they have no clues, you may have to intervene and suggest strategies that you have learned in your exploration.

When Kathy was spending too much time daydreaming and not enough time listening to her fifth grade teacher, Kathy's mom asked questions about the particular behavior. "Is there a certain time of day when you notice this behavior?", and "Is there a certain activity that propels Kathy to daydream?", are two examples. While the teacher focused on the problems Kathy's inattentiveness caused - "She doesn't listen to me and she just sits there and stares or disrupts others when she's supposed to be working" - Kathy's mom was able to bring the statements around to specifics. This takes skill, I know, but keep at it. Kathy's mom and teacher figured out that the afternoon and independent work were both problematic no matter what subject was at hand. Together they found some strategies that helped, like pairing Kathy with an appropriate student she could consult during independent work. To combat the afternoon drifting, Kathy's desk was moved closer to the teacher's and away from windows and other distractions. Kathy's mom could have just accepted the teacher's observations, then poured on the extra discipline and consequences at home, but instead she asked, and asked again. Focusing on the specifics of behaviors and where they are coming from can help.

Sharon tells her story of how she did not ask enough questions, thus delaying the help her son desperately needed. Sharon had enrolled Tommy in kindergarten at age five and one-half, hoping that some of his hyperactive behavior would diminish with time. However, it seemed as though his name ended up on the board (the teacher's discipline strategy) more and more each week. He called out, was squirmy, and occasionally had angry outbursts. At conference time, Tommy's teacher suggested that he was just too immature for kindergarten. At that point, Sharon began her exploration. She read about ADD and wondered if that could be part of Tommy's trouble. When she suggested this, Tommy's teacher said, "Oh, no. Tommy's problems are not caused by ADD. I suggest working on his discipline at home." Perhaps this teacher was exhibiting her own ADD Ignorance or Denial here. Sharon left it at that, after all the teacher had more experience with this type of thing, didn't she? Months later with no progress and Tommy's circle of friends and self esteem dropping off, Sharon approached the teacher again. She also asked Tommy's pediatrician. This time the teacher referred her to the school counselor. Finally Tommy was diagnosed with ADD, and in the nick of time, too. His teacher had wanted him to repeat kindergarten with a new teacher. But, with skills remediation (trying new ways instead of just more practice) and a structured treatment program, Tommy graduated to first grade with the rest of the class. Sometimes you have to ask, and ask again.

In all fairness to educators and day care teachers, there are those who just don't know about or understand ADD. They are the ADD ignorant just as we may have been. If your child's teacher (or coach or grandparent for that matter) is among the ADD ignorant, the best thing you can do is recognize it as such, without judgment. Help them move from ignorance into exploration, at their own pace of course, by offering them the information and sources that have helped you to learn about ADD. All you can do is offer. They have to move into the awareness cycle by choice.

You too may find a time when you need to follow this same advice. It's very easy to slip back into a state of denial as you're searching and helping and the journey becomes just too overwhelming. Know that a trip back to denial ("I'm sick of all this effort, for nothing") is a part of facing any challenge, and for some a necessary one. It keeps us considering, weighing the evidence, looking for more convincing ways.

Also, remember to keep asking those questions, again and again. Don't stop just because you think you've found the last word or the best treatment for now. Your child is growing and developing and your plan of action must grow as well. Don't settle for good-enough. Keep using the things you find are effective, but continue to explore for the thing that might be even better. You have to ask and ask again.

Acceptance

This level of awareness will eventually give you strength and focus to begin shaping an action plan that will foster success for your child. Acceptance doesn't mean giving up. It doesn't imply that you wholly agree with what is diagnosed or suggested. Acceptance points to the fact that no matter what the media or helping professionals present as fact, you choose to take responsibility for your child. You've know something wasn't right and you're now prepared to help him overcome that something. With or without the support of teachers or even your family, you accept that somewhere there exists a strategy of treatment and new skills that will lessen the struggle for your child and you're going to find it! Chapter Eight outlines a plan of action that you can use to shape your own plan. But first, about acceptance...

When you accept the ADD challenge, or whatever challenge it is, you're on the way to conquering it. Such a level of acceptance breeds no victim stories. If you cry victim and look for someone else to fix your woes, you may get only a bandage remedy and the deeper wound and its trouble will linger and grow. You can choose to take responsibility for your child, for your family, for yourself.

Thirteen year-old Suzanne became caught in such a victim trap. It can happen easily. Her troubles grew out of inattentiveness and careless work, and that led to frustration and inappropriate behavior. She was able to make average grades through elementary school but middle school brought the challenges of increased independence and a variety of teachers. Suzanne's advisory teacher expressed these concerns and although her father agreed that something must be done, he maintained that it wasn't his problem to fix. He held the school and the teachers solely responsible to improve Suzanne's performance. So, Suzanne continues to struggle along. Her teachers' varied efforts to help her stay focused helps a little, but the thing that would aid her progress most is for her father to accept that he is accountable to make sure his daughter gets the kind of assistance she needs. Suzanne needs her father to help her discover and manage the root of her problems and then to coordinate a plan of action among her teachers.

In our valiant quest to help our children we do need to consider their feelings and pay attention to their cues. Your son's friends will react to him if you're getting to be known around school as Mr. Pain-In-The-Butt-Parent. So, be accountable to your child as well. She will fight you if you're too controlling and ignore you if you're too loud or annoying. Try to maintain a calm disposition (ha!) as you fight. For me emotional control is key, unfortunately it's also my weak spot.

You'll develop all kinds of skills on this journey. You'll learn about some of them in later chapters. Acceptance of your role in managing the ADD affecting your child will help you hone those skills. I do know this - you'll get plenty of practice to do so.

Recycling

You may ask yourself, "Am I in denial again?" Sometimes in a frenzied time it may seem an easier place to be. If these challenges wouldn't exist, you wouldn't have to work so darn hard. "Why can't we just get a break," you sigh. Says Donald (in denial again), father of ten-year-old Adam, "If everyone else would just try to understand the special qualities Adam has, they would put up with his shenanigans like I do." Some days you feel like you're sick of the world, sick of your kid, sick of trying. Next day you feel guilty that you felt that way. Next day you rekindle your spirit and start out on the journey again.

This is all part of that emotional roller coaster ride we're on and a part that the psychological profession calls recycling. Revisiting each level is okay, it can help you uncover things you haven't thought of before and help you move toward a greater acceptance.

Here are some statements that indicate a state of recycling in each level: Ignorance - "I didn't realize my health insurance would cover some of these expenses." Denial - "Oh, my son's ADD is mild." Exploration - "There's just got to be something else that will work at homework time." Acceptance - "Whether you believe it's ADD or not, dear, our daughter needs to learn organization skills and we need to help her."

See how recycling can refuel our insight and help our direction? Go ahead, visit denial or ignorance again if you need to, just don't stay too long.

YOUR CHILD'S OWN STORY

Collect clues and write the story of your child.
Prepare a folder where you can keep any test results,
health screening reports, etc. that your child receives.
Notes from a kindergarten entrance exam? Third grade
assessment scores? Pre-school report cards? Documents
like these can begin to tell a story about your child. Keep
samples of her writing and drawing through the years, too.
I know you have that refrigerator art saved somewhere.
Start writing in a notebook or journal, thinking about his
infancy and growth to now, jotting notes as you recall.
Get out the photo album book for help.

Besides recording the obvious milestones of child
development (crawling, walking, talking) write in the notebook
or in the margins of this book any insight that happens to pop
into your head. It's a technique authors use to develop a
collection of ideas. Believe me, you'll be surprised how these
clues help to piece together the ADD puzzle. Your note about
Scotty's excellent behavior at his sister's high school musical
may point to his strength as a musical learner, perhaps. In any
case, start writing your child's story right now.

_____'s Story

Your Child's Diagnosis

So here you are, wondering if ADD is the thing that is wreaking havoc in your family. How do we know for sure? Well, there's no single procedure that reveals a positive ADD diagnosis. Blood test? Nope. Throat culture? No way. Genetic testing? Huh - uh. As a matter of fact, there really is no primary medical or behavioral hub for ADD related diagnosis and treatment. It takes clues and notations from many people who interact with your child. You need to seek assistance from your child's teachers, coaches, caregivers, school counselors and psychologists, and medical doctors. The roles of each were discussed in Chapter Two. Together, you will form a team of associates who can help make an appropriate determination if ADD is the root of difficulties for your child. It is normally the child's pediatrician who makes the professional diagnosis. The pediatrician begins with a physical exam to ascertain if any other factors may be affecting your child. Things like ear infections, vision or hearing problems can all affect behavior. The exam will factor out any such contributors. It is important to begin with your child's medical professional because, hopefully, she is the main advisor for your child's total health picture. Still, you will need to consult with others to complete the diagnosis.

The pediatrician can also provide behavioral questionnaires that you can distribute to your child's teachers, caregivers and others. Such a questionnaire is usually completed by rating the existence and level of certain behaviors exhibited by your child. In other words, does Janie call out answers out of turn, how often, and is it a real problem? If your pediatrician does not have access to such surveys, your school psychologist will. I have included samples of such surveys in the Resource Section. My sample may be a bit different than some you've seen, but the idea is to collect information that will aid a diagnosis, and for that purpose the sample will work fine. The pediatrician will most likely suggest behavior modification plans and may prescribe medical treatment for your child. She can also refer you to a counselor or psychologist who can assist parents in verifying a diagnosis and in creating a workable plan to help overcome the difficulties your child experiences as a result of ADD.

School Testing

Many parents first notice a child's frustration with the onset of the early school years. This may be evident since the structure of the school day tends to place greater demands on a child's attention and self-control. And too, the associated ADD symptoms now turn serious if a child's learning potential is hampered. After all, if it's unacceptable behavior we've been facing, we can just stay home for the weekend, right? The problems don't hide as easily in the classroom.

Since ADD is recognized by law as a disability, schools have a responsibility to provide testing services for students who are suspected of having ADD and/or learning disabilities. Ask your child's teacher or school psychologist about your school's policy on when you can obtain testing for your child.

Some of the assessments that can be provided are intelligence tests, academic potential testing, developmental abilities, and social and emotional observations. The results of any of these assessments are used in combination to rule out ADD as a factor, or to determine its part in a child's trouble. It is important to have these assessments completed because the results may uncover other factors such as a learning disability that has been masked or mislabeled as ADD. More on school intervention in Chapter Six, what you need to remember for now is that schools can provide such testing and are required to do so.

Here's the stinger though - there might be a very, very long list of students scheduled for testing and it may take a long time until your child's name comes up. So, I just got off the phone with the principal at my son's school. Joey's teacher and reading specialist agree that there is something in addition to ADD that is affecting his ability to learn to read. The principal said she would put him on "the list" but that he probably won't be tested until around May. It is now February. Would you wait? No, me either. First step is the pediatrician, again. Some alternatives to consider if you face a delay in getting services that you need from your school are: private testing done by a professional not associated with the school, testing by the school district in which you live if your child attends a private school, testing provided by other school districts within your region or state, testing by colleges offering majors in education as sometimes they need test subjects to give their own students practical experience.

TESTS FOR TEACHERS

Questionnaires that are geared specifically for teaching professionals can help to diagnose your child's ADD by pinpointing particular problem areas. One such questionnaire is the Conners' Rating Scale, developed by scientist Dr. Keith Conners, which asks the teacher to rate the degree of a listed problem on a scale of 0 (not at all) to 3 (very much). Problems listed are grouped together in areas of hyperactivity, social skills, emotional maturity, and inattention, though the areas are not labeled as such. You will find a sample of this type of questionnaire in the Resource Section. The results should be reviewed by your team of helpers. This is yet another way to gather information on the way to a diagnosis of ADD.

Who Will Pay?

You may be wondering who will pay for all these specialists and tests. Research you do on your own, for example, can cost nothing if you have access to a well stocked library or parent research collection at your child's school. Many community services like meetings, support groups, and workshops are provided free of charge or for a small fee. When it comes to diagnosis, counseling and remediation there are fees attached that will be billed to someone. If testing and remediation is administered by the school you will probably not see any charges. This includes private schools and some developmental programs too, as long as they are accredited or funded in any way by their state's education department. If the school had agreed to test your child but hasn't gotten around to him in due time, you might be able to recoup your expenses if the school suggests you enlist private testing services.

All this testing and remediation will be provided on the school's terms of course. Jan tells how her daughter was denied testing for a math learning disability, "The teacher and the principal both disputed the trouble Samantha was having with math. They said she had a 'bad attitude' and just needed to 'try harder.' My request for testing was not approved. I ended up switching Samantha to a new school where they tested her and indeed found a problem. I was unwilling to have her stay at her old school and go through the hassle of negotiating, actually fighting, for testing while losing valuable time." So, you still may need to obtain services in the private sector. Your pediatrician most likely charges between $25.00 and $50.00 for an office visit. A private psychologist might charge up to $100.00 per hour for counseling sessions, plus separate fees for testing which can run into hundreds of dollars. Private tutoring or learning centers charge either by the hour or for a pre-determined number of "packaged sessions." Their bill can range from $25.00 per hour up, to hundreds of dollars per package.

How To Pay For Private Services

While the fees of medical, learning and psychological professionals will vary depending on your locale, some also vary fees based on family income. In any case, if you are not receiving services through some type of public assistance or medical card, you will be facing some medical bills. However, most medical insurance do provide coverage for many of the services that your child will need. Check your medical insurance policy to learn what fees are reimbursed, or covered up front. Most policies cover office visits and medication prescribed, sometimes subject to a deductible or co-payment. In addition many plans provide coverage for counseling sessions and treatment at approved counseling centers. I conducted a simple phone survey, calling several health plan providers. While most supplied coverage for office visits and counseling, none of the plans had a benefit that paid for private testing or treatment for behavioral or learning problems. "That's the school's responsibility" I was told. I suppose that is a logical response, and one way for insurance companies to hold the line on costs. But, your child is your responsibility and if you aren't able to get the school to provide the testing that you need in a speedy manner (or not at all), you may want to find room in your budget for private testing. Then, you can approach the school to provide proper remediation if private testing revealed a problem. The timeliness of that remediation will still be a factor. So, keep a line of your household budget open just in case you need to fund private remediation as well.

By now you should have a fair idea of how we find out about ADD, how we don't and why we must. If you're still suspecting ADD as a factor for your child, you learned some ways to begin your search. The next chapter focuses on a variety of treatments for ADD. Here's hoping you'll discover the something that works for your child.

HOW TO PAY... Maybe

Another possibility to help you pay for services is through funding provided by the Social Security Administration under its programs for children with special needs. These special needs categories do include behavioral problems, thus making a child with an ADD diagnosis eligible for Supplemental Security Income (SSI), depending on severity and family income. Ask your doctor or call the Social Security Administration in your area for guidelines. If a child with disabilities is denied SSI benefits strictly due to parental income, he may be then eligible for Medical Assistance (MA) benefits in some states. Depending on the severity of the disability, some states will issue an MA card that provides payment for certain medical benefits such as therapy, prescriptions, physicians' visits, etc. Contact your county assistance office for information. You will need to verify that SSI benefits were denied due to parental income.

Good Luck!

4

TREATMENT METHODS: CHOOSE YOUR WEAPONS

Goals of Treatment

In your search to discover an effective, acceptable treatment plan for your child, first understand that different treatments have particular roles and outcomes. While a disorder such as diabetes may have a variety of treatment options, most have a similar outcome or goal - to artificially balance the amounts of sugar in the body.   Not so with ADD treatments. Here too there are many options, but *the outcome of each is varied, claiming (at least) one of three goals in what they offer in their role of helping our children control the effects ADD.* I prefer to categorize treatments by what they strive to accomplish: *1) accommodate the ADD child 2) minimize the effects ADD has on the child   3) cure (free the child of) ADD.*   So while medication may fall under the *minimize effects* category,   behavior modification could be classified *accommodation* and some physical therapy methods a *cure*.

By understanding these outcomes you will be better able to evaluate a possible treatment plan by determining what it strives (or does not strive) to do. In addition, you will be able to more closely match your child's needs at present and for the future, with treatments that offer a compatible solution. For example, as one parent works toward an ADD diagnosis for his son Andy, Andy needs help *now* to help him stay on task at school - diagnosis or not.   Creating a stimulus-free individual work station in the classroom (accommodation) may provide less distraction (the desired outcome) for now, while other treatments and Andy's needs are being assessed.   The combination of a particular treatment's outcome matched with your child's specific needs begins to form the action plan for your child that we have been working toward. It will all come together in time. First, let's work on understanding the roles of Accommodation, Minimize Effects, and Cure.

Accommodation

Treatment plans that aim to *recognize particular ADD effects that are especially troubling, then introduce methods or situations to move toward success in new ways can be classified accommodation.*   Many ADD texts use the term behavior modification to explain efforts that change a resulting behavior without using medication. But, accommodation is so much more than just modifying a child's behavior. It includes efforts to modify ourselves (the way we perceive and judge a child) and to find ways to adapt a child's external environment, as well as the focus on changing (or modifying) a child's resulting behavior.

External Means of Accommodating

One mother shares a classic accommodation method that most of us suspecting ADD will encounter, and those of us with ADD kids routinely see each new school year.   "I felt a sinking feeling in my heart when I attended Back-To-School night to meet my daughter Jessie's third grade teacher - only to find Jessie's desk smack up against the teacher's desk. I moaned, 'Not already' as the teacher motioned to me to stay after the rest of the parents." You've been there, too?   If you haven't you most likely will be.

This classic accommodation, where the child's environment is adapted (the desk is placed strategically to minimize distraction), may be one of your first clues!

In another scenario, when he couldn't get his son Ryan to get himself out of bed in the morning, this dad resorted to setting several annoying alarm clocks to go off within minutes of each other. And, the alarms kept on ringing until Ryan shut them off, not Dad. Other timers signaled points in time when Ryan should be eating, washing, packing his backpack, heading out the door, etc. If this dad wanted to also include behavior modification in his accommodation, he could reward Ryan with some motivator (stickers, sports cards, etc.) whenever he made it through all the alarms.

Situation Accommodation

Sometimes we have to take a closer look at the troubling situation our child happens to be in, and consider if the solution lies not with our child but with the situation itself.

Tyler's mom talks about her realization of suiting particular situations to her six-year-old's personality and challenges. "Tyler loves sports and he's a pretty good athlete. He loves to run and kick, so I thought I was doing right by him when I signed him up for the local soccer league. He made the 'A' team for boys under eight years old and he was having a great time, until the second game. Some parents were shouting orders at their kids. The coaches were shouting, too. If a player made a mistake, the coaches pulled him out right away. Hey, these were six and seven-year-olds having fun on a Saturday morning. This was not the World's Cup! I knew that Tyler's inability to follow directions and remember rules was soon to clash with the coaches' expectations. We didn't need that aggravation. This was supposed to provide fun and success, after all. We found and switched to an intramural soccer program at our local YMCA that suited Tyler much better."

As adults, we have some control in choosing situations our child encounters and we should exercise our choice to adapt when we can. Granted, it's important to have rules both for safety and as a means for children to develop self discipline. However, our world is competitive enough and our children will meet it soon enough. Why hurry? Suit the situation to meet the child's needs.

Accommodation Does Not Mean Punishment

Over the past few years the term behavior modification has mistakenly come to mean punishment. Unfortunately, some who perceive it as such just happen to include teachers, relatives, coaches, and others who interact with our child.

While the following example is at the extreme end of how society misinterprets behavior modification, it is not a rare occurrence by any means: *Hard Copy* had aired a story in May of 1996 about use of an isolation box for misbehavior in school. The box, it said, was being used in a significant number of primarily Texan schools mainly for misbehavior. The box measured 4' x 4' x 7'. There was a little window in the door but many children were too short and couldn't see out the window. School policy dictated that misbehaved kids should only be in the box for minutes at a time. However, the show reported that one boy was kept in the box for much longer than that, one time for 2 hours!

Whether or not the story was exaggerated is besides the point. It is a prime example of behavior modification wrongly utilized. For behavior modification to be effective, *the focus must be on finding effective ways and adapting situations in a positive manner to help children cope with effects caused by ADD.* We should think of these ways and adaptations as strategies for success, not as means for disciplinary action.

The use of consequences (for our discussion, the natural or logical outcomes of negative or unacceptable actions) has been promoted as the nineties method of discipline. One overused example is that if a child dawdles and misses the bus, he finds his own way to school. (Yeah, right...) However, consequences are not really accommodations. Sure, you may argue that several pink slips leading to detention should indeed modify a child's behavior. But, our ADD kids don't usually make the connection between their actions and the outcome - and that connection is essential for consequences to be effective.

Case in point - Judy was only eight years old when she received her first formal disciplinary warning, a pink slip, from the teacher. When discussing the warning with her mother, Judy readily admitted to doodling cartoons during a class lecture. "Mom," she said "the teacher was just up there blabbing away. We weren't doing anything important. It was boring. I was just drawing ideas for my science report, what's the big deal anyway?" Judy's mother proceeded to explain the importance of paying attention to a speaker, whether in a classroom, church or business meeting, whether we're bored or not. Together they played a game where she presented Judy with a number of things that could claim her attention when the teacher was lecturing: other students in the hall, noise from the street outside, the snack in her desk for recess, an urge to doodle, etc. Judy was to pick the thing that *deserved* her attention at the moment - not the one she thought was best, or most interesting. She explained that Judy could use this technique during school whenever she caught herself wandering.

Dr. Mel Levine, in his book *Keeping A Head In School* (Educators' Publishing Service 1990), teaches such a technique by suggesting that our mind is like a television set offering many channels to choose from, but that only one choice is appropriate for any given time. Maybe, just maybe, Judy could learn to choose the appropriate channel too. Back to connections... Judy did end up serving an afternoon in detention for receiving three pink slips for a variety of offenses throughout the marking period. And even though the resulting consequence was spending the detention hour writing about her offenses and how she could handle these situations in the future, Judy met her mother at the door afterwards with a big grin announcing "Mom, that was kind of fun!" Missing connection? Uh huh.

This is just one example of why we ADD parents need to be careful not to rely too heavily on consequences in our accommodation methods, especially those "natural" or "logical" consequences that are supposed to occur to our children without much thought or resolve, but don't.

Encouraging the Positive

Other accommodation techniques focus on encouraging the positive and ignoring the not-so-positive. Miss Sally, a first grade teacher, keeps a large jar on the shelf for all to see. When students complete tasks on time, quietly, etc., they can add buttons to the jar. An ADD student in the class who is able to sustain attention for certain intervals adds buttons for his contribution to the class. A full jar of buttons is rewarded with extra recess time, an additional story, or some other motivator. Effective for most students, this short term reward system can work well especially for the ADD child. While some teachers include a negative consequence with this type of system; not completing tasks on time results in buttons being taken out for example; focusing on the positive tends to be the more effective method.

Stanley I. Greenspan, author of *The Challenging Child* (Addison-Wesley, 1995) and Mary MacCracken, author of *Turnabout Children* (Little, Brown & Co., 1986) both suggest that at least fifty percent of our efforts should be aimed at encouraging our children's strengths and positive actions. The other fifty percent can be spent on developing their weak spots. Usually we spend in excess of 50% on the negative stuff. Whoops. Greenspan calls it the *50% Rule*. However, it's not as easy as it sounds. Just think about how much time we (I'm guilty too) spend judging and correcting our children versus the time we spend noticing the things they do right. The *50% Rule* is something we can do to modify our own behavior within our plan to accommodates our children in a respectful way.

More Rewards for the Positive

What about our ADD kids and the popular use of reward systems using charts, stickers and so forth? Many child psychology experts encourage us to provide a reward system for our children. This fits nicely with the idea of complimenting our children at least fifty percent of the time. Just a caution - while reward systems like goal charts are used in many parenting programs, they are *not the only* behavior modification method available.

Here's what Marty, father of ten-year-old Brett had to share. "I tape a chart to the fridge. It lists a number of behaviors and actions that we're trying to encourage such as, didn't interrupt others on phone, asked to use others' belongings, and so on. I originally had spaces for one week's worth of performance, but it wasn't too long that I discovered that a week was just too long a time for Brett to go without some recognition or reward. So, I changed it to a one day deal with his choice of a small reward like a baseball card, or chips he could use towards something bigger like a movie rental. We continuously negotiate the rewards to keep it interesting. I used to dole out penalty points for negative behavior but that didn't seem to be as effective. This chart idea was the first thing that was suggested to me as a way to deal with ADD and I tried using it for months. Now I have learned other methods, so I only use the chart every few weeks since Brett gets bored with it. Another thing I have to watch out for is Brett's little sister, Caitlyn, sabotaging the chart. Even though I put up a chart for her too, it's just too tempting to mess with his. When I see this happening I put the charts away for awhile and try something else."

Varying Your Accommodation Methods

I have presented here just some examples of accommodation ideas; more are offered in chapters five (school related) and eight (behavior related). The point is that accommodating our children is somewhat simple and a very caring way to ease their frustrations, and their caretakers' frustrations too. The challenge is to be creative in thinking of new ways to adapt to problem situations. You'll need to review and revise your methods because what works one day will get old and become ineffective after a time. Ask your child for suggestions. He may come up with just the thing. My own son, Joey, is a rough riser just like Ryan whom you met earlier. Sometimes I ask him, "Joey how should I wake you up tomorrow?" Sometimes he asks to be tickled awake, to have the dog jump on him, or some other crazy way. But he never, *never* asks to be constantly nagged in a witch's voice repeating "Get up, get up get up!"

Remember that while these efforts help to modify behavior, *ADD and its effects don't go away permanently through accommodation;* that's not its role after all. The wonderful thing about accommodating a child is that it can provide opportunity for success without medication or negative feedback. And, you can pick and choose the particular effects or situations that need modifying - the fidgeting has got to stop during math class, but that extra energy is a plus on the soccer field. Don't lose the good stuff!

Accommodation is also useful because you can employ it when you are first beginning your trek toward an ADD diagnosis. Once you have enough evidence to support your suspicion and get that diagnosis, you can begin to consider other methods to minimize effects or move towards a cure. Meanwhile, helping your child meet his present needs through accommodation; be it teaching him self-control strategies or having teacher check her listing of homework assignments; shows loving support that is so important, ADD or not.

Minimize Effects

Another treatment outcome is the minimization of ADD effects. *Treatment plans that attempt to minimize or temporarily prevent the resulting effects of ADD include things like prescription medications, diet intervention, and home and natural remedies.* These treatments propose to relieve the child (and interacting others) of the classic ADD problem behaviors like inattentiveness, impulsivity, hyperactivity, etc. The minimization of these problem behaviors in turn may provide opportunity for the child to practice self-control, concentration, focus, and so on.

The use of treatments designed to minimize effects should not be confused as an ADD cure. While some are very effective for many children, the treatments are effective only when used consistently. Normally, when the medication, diet intervention or natural remedy is stopped, the results also stop. Unlike an ear infection, for example, once you treat with antibiotics, the infection in time goes away. Not so with ADD. Most physicians and psychologists agree that ADD itself does not go away. While it may seem to decrease in intensity over the years, these experts guess that this is most likely due to the child's efforts in learning to deal effectively with her ADD problem areas. Certainly then, controlling the effects of ADD can help a child to deal with his own resulting behaviors, ultimately driving a child's success as well.

Ways to Minimize Effects

While I certainly agree that we parents put a lot of effort into finding ways to prevent certain behaviors from erupting in our children, thus minimizing some undesirable outcomes, I place those efforts in the accommodation category, mainly because they involve finding new ways to handle predictable situations. When we seek to minimize effects of ADD, we face the fact that we can't always ward off the ADD with accommodation only, and knowing what results are inevitable we strive to ease those results.

In researching a variety of approaches to minimize the effects of ADD, most can be grouped as: prescription medications; diet, nutrition and environmental intervention; or natural (non-chemical) and home remedies. First, you need to learn more about these approaches. I present an overview of each and include resources for further research. Second, you should discuss any approach with your child's doctor. Finally, choose to use or not use them based on what you've learned and discussed and paired with your child's needs and the benefits that the treatments may provide.

Prescription Medication

Why start here? Well, the use of prescription medications in the treatment of ADD is the most widely accepted among the medical profession. This does not mean that getting your physician to prescribe medication is an easy task. Remember our discussion in the last chapter about how a child is ultimately diagnosed as ADD? Because ADD is indeed difficult and time consuming to diagnose, a prescription for medication to treat it may be a long time in coming. No one wants a child to be medicated unnecessarily. With this in mind, insurance companies that offer plans covering the costs of prescription medications are very particular about the steps that need to be taken to prove an ADD diagnosis and its treatment. Besides wanting to control the cost of insurance premiums through refusing to reimburse costs of unnecessary items, many carriers cite a genuine concern for children's health as a reason for such strict processes.

The Decision to Treat

If your child suffered from diabetes, for example, you wouldn't hesitate to administer medication, most likely insulin, to minimize the ill effects on her behalf. Further, most of society would judge you an unfit parent if you didn't. However, when it comes to the treatment of ADD, administering medication (meds) to a child to manipulate behavior is seen as a cop-out by much of society, and they let you know it.

How often have you heard this snide remark (or something along these lines) among a group of parents discussing kids and school. "Oh sure, Johnny is in my Mary's class, and well, you know he's hard to handle. Why, he goes to the nurse every lunch hour for a dose of downers just so he'll behave ." Ouch. Hurts doesn't it? It hurts me to hear remarks like that about other kids as much as if I'd hear it about my own. I usually offer a come-back like, "Gee I really feel for Johnny. He must find it really tough to live with all the criticism he gets..." Or, here's one that helps to change the subject - "Wow, what do you say about my kid when I'm not around?" Anyway, we'll discuss your handling of such judgment later. I bring this subject up to point out just how cruel others can be as you try to treat your child's ADD. Somehow, ADD is not socially justifiable as a medical illness, and so treating it with meds becomes questionable as well.

Just as the diabetic in our earlier example would surely suffer without proper medical treatment, so might our ADD children. The stigma that surrounds the medicating of ADD children often keeps us from discovering the benefits that properly prescribed, administered, and monitored meds can provide. *The benefits come not from the meds themselves, but from a child who now has some control over himself.* While no pharmaceutical manufacturer, physician or psychologist would promise that prescription medicines in the treatment of ADD *make* a child pay attention, choose appropriate actions or stop annoying others for example, these groups do suggest that the medications can enhance a child's *ability* to choose her actions and where her attention is focused, thus providing *opportunity* for successful outcomes. So, in that light, Suzy may still *choose* to tune out the teacher and tune into some distraction, but without the medication, her ability to choose to focus may be weak or non-existent.

How do meds do this? As introduced in Chapter 2, medical experts theorize that meds act as chemical messengers, energizing the brain's metabolism rate and helping it to use glucose at a more effective rate. These chemical messengers send a "wake up call" to that area of the brain responsible for responses such as filtering ability and self-control. The term *neurotransmitter,* used in many ADD texts, *is a naturally occurring chemical messenger;* in other words the human body makes it, at least in those who are not ADD. *Dopamine,* which sounds like a med but is not, is a naturally occurring molecule of the neurotransmitter. So, prescription medications are often said to supplement the body's creation of neurotransmitters, increasing the number and frequency of messages sent to that special area of the brain that for ADD children has been inactive or underactive, until now.

The benefits meds can provide are based on improved self-control (controlling impulsive behavior and hyperactivity) and filtering ability (choosing from a number of distractions.) The result then is the minimization of bothersome effects like talking out of turn, making rude noises, daydreaming, running wild, etc. The minimization of these effects then help to provide opportunity for success and give the child the ability to make appropriate choices.

But, what about side effects from meds? Side effects are a possibility that you must consider with the use of prescription meds, or for that matter, any treatment which introduces or changes elements that the body ingests and uses.

I get into specific side effects in the explanations of the different types of prescription meds available. For now, know that side effects can include those related to both physical and mental health. Some common complaints from meds treatment include stomach upset, mood swings, and decreased appetite. Some side effects can be controlled by adjusting the dosage or the combination of medications. Some side effects may diminish over time while some might occur only after sustained use. Look for further information in your library under "medications" or ask your pharmacist. Many pharmacies offer a computer station where you can use a touch screen to obtain a print-out of information about a variety of prescription medicines. Not all children experience side effects, but you do need to be aware of the possibility.

Finally, after learning about and considering both the advantages and disadvantages of using meds as a treatment to minimize ADD effects, how to ultimately decide on their use? Think about how ADD affects your child both at home and at school - academically and socially. Make a chart. In one column list the effects; could be both positive or negative. Next, rate the effects in order or importance 0 - 4. A rating of 0 would mean that the effect is one that is welcome or tolerable - her ability to scope out the whole situation or his athletic energy. A rating of 4 would mean something that greatly impairs her functioning or causes inexcusable behavior - his inability to keep his hands to himself or her lack of self-control that turns to stealing. In the next columns note ways that you have attempted to accommodate your child and the results + or -. Also jot down any ways that ADD has affected the family - the marriage is strained or the siblings are crying injustice!

Effects Rating vs. Method Results

EFFECT	RATING 0-4 (0 = no problem, 4 = greatly impairs)	ACCOMO- DATION METHOD	RESULTS + / -
Can't keep hands to herself….	3	*Moved her desk away from others*	-
Daydreams during seatwork, can't stay focused.	4	*Teacher taps on shoulder .*	+ **but limited**
Aware of surroundings and quick reflexes	0	*Great for soccer! Remembers details.*	**Don't change this!**

Here's a blank list for you to try…

EFFECT	RATING 0-4 0 = no problem 4 = greatly impairs	ACCOMO- DATION METHOD	RESULTS + / -

Now look at the list you've made and note the real trouble areas and what you've done to ease them. Consider what the minimization of such effects would mean.

If your child would benefit in light of the possibility of side effects or social stigma that taking meds could cause, by all means consider treatment. If, on the other hand, you judge the possibility of side effects or social snubbing to be far worse than the ADD effects your child is dealing with, consider more methods of accommodation while searching for a cure. Weigh the options depending on your child and your family's needs.

Dr. Greenspan, introduced earlier, suggests medication only "if the effects are seriously hampering life relationships, etc." But, only you can decide just what "seriously hampering" means. Another "right choice" for you to make...

Certainly, we should consider these same types of options and weigh the positives versus the negatives for any of the treatments outlined. However, when it comes to prescription meds for children, the social label turns the helpful medication into a "drug" and so our need for knowledge and our duty to our children seem heavier.

Options to Try

If you're still on the fence when considering meds for your child, think about easing into a treatment plan, or adjusting the meds to your child's needs. Depending on the particular med that your child's doctor has prescribed, you may not have to adhere to a strict three-times-a-day (for example) routine.

Some parents may find success in, depending on the med, medicating only for specific situations or time frames. For example, nine-year-old Sara takes meds only during school hours, Monday through Friday and September through June. Time released meds may be an option, especially for the child who is concerned about social/peer pressure that taking meds at school may provoke. Seven-year-old Nathan takes just one dose in the morning during school days. It seems to be enough to get him through most of his "boring subjects" as he calls them. The afternoon includes more appealing activities such as lunch, recess, and specials like gym, art or music. Nathan is able to stay in control for those!

Thirteen-year-old Alana has found that she benefits from meds most during her menstrual cycle and just before. Her mother agrees that this hormonal and ADD combination is just a bit too much for Alana to handle all at once, and an increased dosage of meds can ease this trying time. Note that there can be problems such as mood swings, drop in blood pressure, etc. with starting and stopping some meds though, so you must check with your doctor or pharmacist before attempting any of these options.

Dr. S., a psychologist that my family has worked with, would rather see parents persist with the accommodation methods, but he does agree that meds can be beneficial for some children. He suggests using meds as a starting point in low doses to aid the child in beginning to find success. Meanwhile, he stresses that it is important to help the child learn about her own challenges and focus on ways to balance those effects. Dr. S points out, "Don't discount the amazing ability children have to self-monitor - to 'catch themselves'- concerning their behaviors and feelings. Meds can help this along while they're on their own learning curve. But, they must strengthen their self motivation on their own and with your help; meds won't do it for them."

So, you may want to start thinking about meds as an aid to helping your child deal with her ADD effects, rather than as the end-treatment.

The Prescription Medications

The meds most commonly prescribed and available for minimizing the effects of ADD are usually grouped into three main categories: Stimulants, Hypertension Aides and Anti-Depressants.

Stimulants, or amphetamines, seem to work on ADD's effects by energizing the middle brain enough to provide the child the ability to control his physical actions(hyperactivity) and mental sensations (focus).

Hypertension Meds, like clonidine which has been used to treat high blood pressure for over twenty years, have been found to reduce the extreme level of excitement in the very hyperactive ADD child, although they do not help to improve distractibility.

Some anti-depressants, those that are tricyclic (of a certain chemical structure), are thought to ease ADD's effects by improving mood, impulsivity, and frustration tolerance. However, the anti-depressants seem to have less affect on attention control.

Following, you will find a discussion listing the type of med, it's brand and generic names, and possible side effects. Note that manufacturers must list side effects even when rare or found in a very small sampling. If the possibility of a particular side effect should cause you alarm, research the med more completely. A complete medicine guide, your pharmacist or doctor, or the manufacturer can provide information on the med's testing and results. What you learn may or may not help your decision to try a particular med.

Concerning side effects, Ph.D.s Ingersoll and Goldstein site cases where parents and physicians may conclude, in error, that some problems are actually side effects, when indeed the problems have "gone unnoticed or unremarked upon until medication has been introduced." They report that in studies of children taking either a placebo (containing no medicine) or Ritalin, some so-called side effects, like irritability and excessive staring are essentially the same under both conditions. These results were reported by R.A. Barkley in the *Clinical Child Psychology Newsletter* 3; (1989).

You may have heard, from other ADD parents and other sources, about additional meds that I have not chosen to list here. Be careful when investigating these other meds. Many times our ADD kids are also suffering from depression, emotional disorders, learning disabilities, and so on. Keep clear in your mind what effects you are striving to minimize. Yes, doctors may prescribe certain combinations of meds to treat the effects of several disorders. But *you* will need to be vigilant about what meds are helping to ease the effects of which disorder, and which meds seem to have no affect, or are in fact causing more harm than good.

The Stimulants
Ritalin (methylphenidate) Most widely prescribed in the treatment of ADD. Doctors try Ritalin first in most cases because it has good results in most children. Side effects that may go away during treatment include decrease in appetite, stomach ache, sense of sadness. Long term may include liver damage in rare cases. In most cases it is relatively safe to miss or stop doses for weekend, vacations, etc. Some children may experience whininess or mood changes when med wears off at days' end. Available in 5mg, 10 mg and 20 mg tablets.

Ritalin SR (methylphenid sustained release): Similar to Ritalin but in a time released formula. Offers longer (1 - 3 hours) term effectiveness, in some cases eliminating need for school hour dose. Available in 10 mg and 20 mg, but not very suitable for breaking for half doses due to the time release component.

Adderal (dextroamphetamine) which is commonly used for narcolepsy (a rare condition marked by excessive sleepiness): Adderal is an updated combination of stimulants, approved by the FDA in 1996, and providing a longer lasting effect. Similar to Ritalin, but has an effective life of 6-8 hours in many cases, eliminating the need for the school hour dose. Some children will experience less mood swings than Ritalin when dose wears off. Side effects may include dry mouth, unpleasant taste, constipation, loss of appetite and nervousness. Tablet is scored (has a groove across the middle of the tablet) for half doses. Available in 10mg and 20 mg.

Cylert (magnesium pemoline): A stimulant that works similar to Ritalin, but structured differently. Usually tried if Ritalin has poor results. Need for kidney testing and monitoring - long term use may affect kidney functioning. May ease side effects like stomach ache and decreased appetite that are associated with Ritalin. Nervousness, trouble sleeping, and headaches may result. Available in 10 mg and 20 mg.

The Anti-Depressants
Imipramine Used in combination with stimulants if depression is noted. Not normally used for treatment of ADD alone. Can be fatal in large doses. Possible dry mouth, constipation and drowsiness. Patient must be monitored through use of electrocardiogram (EKG) . Medication must be withdrawn gradually to avoid possible flu-like symptoms associated with abrupt withdrawal.

The Hypertension Meds (Blood pressure medication)
Clonidine (methyldopa) Can affect blood pressure adversely, · may cause drowsiness in large doses, dry mouth, constipation,

or depression. Must be increased gradually as well as withdrawn gradually to avoid stress on the heart and blood pressure. Often taken in combination with anti depressants.

Others - fact or faux?

<u>Dopamine</u> - Not a med. This is a naturally occurring neurotransmitter molecule.

<u>Dramamine</u> - for treatment of anti-motion sickness. Suggested by and based on the theories of Dr. Levinson (see Chapter 2), to correct an imbalance of the inner ear and CVS system.

<u>Benydryl, Triaminic, Dimeatapp:</u> antihistamines normally used to relieve symptoms of the cold virus and/or allergies. Also suggested by and based on Levinson's theory.

Parents Talk About Meds

Sometimes parents report a world of difference in their child within days or even hours with meds. The dosage and combination of meds is very crucial. Still, let's not medicate if the results are not prime. On the other hand, lets not perhaps further complicate our child's life by allowing her to suffer when quite possibly a carefully monitored med program will ease her troubles.

Here are some comments from parents on both sides of the issue, offering their opinions and experiences. Know that each child responds differently. I provide these comments so that you may get a feel for the variety and wide array of possibilities. Comments have been gathered from support groups, surveys, and public information sources.

No one can force you to medicate your kids. The decision belongs to you. However, I do not understand why many parents are against it. Proper medication in carefully adjusted doses gives great results for many kids (though there are some that do not respond to medication...)

My concerns are for the use of drugs - their adverse side effects and extended health risks down the road in years to come. It is clear to me that drugs are far from safe for our children. I will keep searching for a better avenue for dealing with this problem.

My 9 year-old son takes 25mg of Ritalin on school days. He takes 10 mg in the morning, 10 mg at midday, and 5 mg after school. On weekends or when school is not in session, he takes 5 mg three times a day. Occasionally during long vacations from school, when both my wife and I are able to cope, we don't bother with it at all and let him rip! I was originally resistant to my wife's idea of "drugging" our son. However his life, and mine, has improved greatly since the Ritalin. His academic performance has improved too. He has gone from a non-reader to the top reading group in his class. He has more friends now.

I'm sure most parents are competent enough to know that their children won't benefit from medication...

It's not that I am entirely happy with the need for drug therapy, but the benefits are so significant. I would feel more guilty withholding the medication from my child.

I think a lot of us feel a twinge of doubt about giving our children controlled substances.

The Ritalin guilt-thing is probably part of the process of mourning the loss of a "normal" child.

A parent's decision whether to use or not use med therapy is very personal and must be respected.

I confess that I am not made of the stuff that would permit me to effectively parent my daughter without some help from meds. Sometimes this feels like my failure.

A kid on the proper medication is able to focus at an appropriate level and can complete his school tasks, if there are no accompanying disabilities.

We went on vacation this summer and ran out of his medication the last two days. It was like having two different children...

I got the best support on this from my sister. She cannot get anything accomplished in a day without her medication. Don't feel bad about giving it.

To me ADD is a gift, and structuring that gift is one hard thing to do. I have improved the structure for myself and am trying to give my son my complete understanding of ADD. Not by being easygoing, but by him getting exercise, social activities, extra learning time right after school, and most important - finding the right medication.

Q. It is so frustrating to find the right medications in the right doses. It is also pretty scary. We resisted meds for so long, but now I'm beginning to wonder if maybe we were right all along. I feel like I'm playing roulette with my child.
A.. Don't give up looking and trying for that right thing. Something will work out along the way, and after all, a less frustrating, more successful life for your child is the goal

and the pursuit of that is always worth it. The road is long and hard but you'll find the way that is best for your family, because you care.

There is a study on people who have taken Ritalin for 45 years which showed no, absolutely no, ill effects. Ask your pharmacist.

My son started out with regular Ritalin but it seemed erratic. He now takes 20 mg time-released Ritalin in the morning and 10mg of regular Ritalin in the afternoon. He seems to have much fewer "peaks and valleys", more level in his behavior. And, his appetite is much improved. The results have been positive.

We have used Adderal for months with our son and believe it is effective. The good things are it's long lasting, he doesn't lose his appetite, it's one pill not two. Bad thing is when he "crashes"; the 30-60 minute come down period can be rough if it's a conflict situation. After that he's a normal loving child.

My child has been on a combination of Cylert and Prozac. Our doctor thinks that combining the two is a good option for a lot of kids. His explanation to me was that when they become more focused with the stimulant sometimes things that didn't bother then before now do. This causes them to be anxious and sometimes depressed. That's what our doctor said anyway.

I don't know if Clonidine will work for all - but it is a God send for me and my child.

Our son was on Ritalin for three years and was VERY ANGRY. A new doctor prescribed the blood pressure medicine clonidine. He started out on a very slow dose and with each minor adjustment the doctor put his teachers through the third degree as to his behaviors. The difference is unbelievable. What a difference a good doctor can make.

My son has been on clonidine for years - he used to take it alone, then with Ritalin, and now only to help him sleep. It is a definite alternative for some kids, but since it is a blood pressure medication we were told to monitor his blood pressure and schedule an electrocardiogram (EKG) once per year. Also we were told to never stop the drug suddenly because of the risk of dropping the blood pressure too quickly.

Being on Ritalin has had very positive effects on my teenage daughter. Her school and I tried various methods before I allowed her to be put on medication and the results were a frustrated child with low self-esteem. Once she was on the correct dose her ability to concentrate in school improved immediately. Periodically her meds have to be adjusted but we have never come anywhere close to the "zombie" stage that I was afraid of in the beginning. She is basically a happier child on medication - still too mouthy, but functioning well.

My son may not need meds forever, but of course I wouldn't promise him that.

My child takes Cylert and it works well. In some cases it is associated with problems with liver enzymes and functions, so we had to have a baseline liver function test done and regular (every six months) liver function tests.

When I was training to be an educator...one of the things that was always pressed was to encourage the parents not to seek the "fast-food" cure, i.e. medication ONLY. Rather that when medication was indicated, to also gently suggest therapy if not for the aiding of the transition into a medication, for the transition into more of a normalcy. As parents we also need to switch gears and aid our kids in that arena - to suddenly have more patience, longer attention span, the ability to stop and rationalize what's happening, as if we too are now in a different world...

For two years I gave my daughter only a 5 mg morning dose of Ritalin on school days - figuring that was the responsible thing to do, and also lessening my guilt. I now have agreed to a midday dose and sometimes an after school dose too. The benefits are so, so positive for her - now I feel like I cheated her those two years!

The ultimate decision whether to try meds therapy is up to you and your child - together.

Nutrition and Diet Intervention

Another possibility to consider to help minimize your child's ADD effects, is an evaluation and modification of her diet and nutritional intake. The basis behind nutritional treatments is to rid the body of any food that is causing discomfort, allergic reaction, etc. that in turn may be causing ill effects. Whether the effects are truly ADD or not, certainly making your child's life more comfortable is good measure in any case. Many nutrition specialists suggest that negative reactions to foods and drinks can cause learning disabilities as well as ADD effects. On the other hand as many other experts, while they agree that diet and nutrition are very important to a child's overall wellness, do not believe that a special or restricted diet improves ADD symptoms.

One of the earliest champions of diet intervention was Dr. Ben Feingold. He found that when treating children for allergic reactions by restricting certain dyes and preservatives from the diet, ADD-like behaviors also improved. Thus, the Feingold Diet emerged. There are those who swear by the Feingold method and use it solely to minimize their children's ADD challenges. Still others use the method in combination with meds and accommodation. But most likely, the largest group includes those who have experimented with the diet and either found complying too difficult, or the results minimal at best. It may be worth a try if yours is one of the 2-4% of children who respond to this method.

How to Test For Food Based Allergies

In her book, *Is This Your Child? Discovering & Treating Unrecognized Allergies* (William Morrow, 1991), Dr. Doris Rapp suggests removing the suspected food or drink from the diet completely for about a week. Then the food should be reintroduced to the child for the next few days, having him eat as much as he wants or more. Careful observations are then recorded at a variety of hours later, noting any critical or subtle changes in behavior or abilities (mood, reading or writing for example). For the next two weeks she suggests testing a different food, and so on until you have found the things that are causing your child his troubles. This may take a long time, but can produce positive findings, Rapp says. She notes that sometimes the very thing that is causing trouble for your child is the food that she craves the most.

Shelly tells how her daughter Tiana asked for strawberry-flavored milk at every opportunity - breakfast, snack, supper, bed time. So, it was strawberry milk that was the first thing that was restricted from Tiana's diet. Shelly described that week of denying the favored drink a pure hassle, a real battle of wills. However, Shelly reported that when reintroducing the beloved strawberry milk, Tiana's bouts with whininess and mood changes drastically increased. Then Shelly realized that she still couldn't be sure of her findings - was it the milk or the strawberry syrup? She then restricted plain milk and dairy products, with similar results. Suspecting a possible dairy intolerance, Shelly scheduled an appointment with Tiana's pediatrician.

If you need help figuring out what to test, check with your doctor or nutritionist for guidance. And although experts in the ADD field do not recommend diet intervention as a sole approach to effectively treating ADD, it may help provide some relief.

Other Environmental Concerns

Besides food allergies, some nutritionists also blame allergic reactions to elements in our environment for the effects of ADD. Dr. Rapp is one such champion of this theory. In her book, Rapp discusses her belief that allergic reactions to a host of things are indeed the root of learning and behavioral disorders, which include ADD. Her work has created a whole new group of "adapted" Feingold followers who believe environmental restrictions, as well as diet intervention is the cure for the cause. Rapp suggests allergy testing for non-food allergy suspicions. This procedure is usually done in the office of a specialist where a variety of elements are introduced to the body by pricking the skin with a bit of the suspected foe. You might be familiar with this testing as a way to discover allergic reactions to different types of pollens or pet dander.

Rapp suggests taking the test a step further by introducing other elements that might be found in the living or school environment as well. Elements from everyday items such as chalk dust, perfumes, laundry products, wall and floor treatments, etc., are examples of possible test candidates. Again, certainly if a child experiences discomfort from any such element, efforts should be made to remove it from the environment. However, we must remember that treating such allergies may only be a small part of minimizing effects for our ADD children.

Sugar: Friend or Foe?

How many of us have been accused of giving our children too many sweets and too much sugar, thus bringing on their hyperactive behavior? I would guess about 99% of us are among the accused. There are many arguments on both sides of the issue. One side says too much sugar causes hyperactivity. The other says it's not the sugar, it's the situations (birthday and holiday parties, etc.) in which sweets are eaten that are the culprits.

Calling it the "sugar factor", *Working Mother* magazine (September 1996) reported the results of two studies aimed at addressing the current disagreement that sugar does/does not cause hyperactivity. In one study conducted at the Yale University School of Medicine, researchers found that when eaten on an empty stomach, high sugar consumption caused shakiness, excitement and lowered concentration in children, the effects taking place *two to five hours later*. Says *WM*, "This suggests that sugar alone makes children more hyperactive - if they haven't had nutritious foods to balance the effects."

The second is a joint study conducted by researchers at the Mellinger Clinic and the University of Kentucky. In contrast to the first findings, this study found that when parents hold a belief that sugar heightens a child's activity level, they expect more overactive behavior. The study included only boys of mothers who believed that sugar would effect their sons' behaviors. The boys were each given a fruit drink and half of the mothers were told the drink had high sugar content while the other half of the mothers were told that the drink contained a sugar substitute. Actually none of the drinks included any sugar.

The boys were observed thirty minutes later, first alone and then with their mothers present. Researchers found that the behavior that changed was that of *the mothers, not the boys.* They found that the boys all played calmly, but that the mothers who thought their sons had a high sugar drink were more critical and controlling. These mothers also remained more physically closer to their sons. The mothers who thought their sons had a sugar-substitute drink were noted as being more friendly and warm toward their sons. Surprising? Probably not to most of us ADD parents.

One father in a support group to which I belong confided to me that he thinks he sometimes makes things worse for his daughter. He says, "I'm kind of a monitor I guess, ready to correct or distract before her behavior gets out of control." The study as reported by *WM* concluded that there *is* a connection between sugar and hyperactivity: "Parents' beliefs about sugar make them more hypervigilant with their children."

In their book Attention Deficit Disorders and Learning Disabilities: Realities, Myths, and Controversial Treatments, (Doubleday, 1993) Ph.D.s Barbara Ingersoll and Sam Goldstein conclude that from many scientific studies testing the theory over the years, findings are not consistent that support the idea that sugar causes hyperactivity. And, although Ingersoll and Goldstein do point out that in rare cases limiting sugar in the diets of children who show an abnormal craving for sugars is appropriate, overall they do not recommend a sugar-restricted diet as an effective approach in the treatment of

ADD. Further, the authors note, "In the daily life of the ADHD child, already fraught with so many problems, it simply does not make sense to use an approach that may provide nothing more than additional opportunities for parent-child conflict." Well said, I think.

A forgotten consideration for those who believe sugar to be the culprit of ADD forget that some of our children suffer from ADD - Inattentive type which includes no hyperactivity in the behavior. Here's the catch phrase aimed at our Inattentive-ADD kids, "I've got to light a fire under that kid..." No sugar there.

Caffeine - Just another stimulant?

Researches agree that caffeine intake, while creating short term energy for some, can actually improve the effects suffered by the ADD child. This goes back to the theory the stimulants wake up the transmitters in the brain, offering the child better focus and self-control.

Some parents report that early treatment methods included serving a caffeinated beverage to their children which indeed did help to provide more focus and less hyperactivity. Caution - do not try this without speaking to your doctor. Caffeine is a stimulant and should be considered a med when used as such, and there's always the possibility of addiction and withdrawal symptoms.

Natural Remedies

It seems that every week I receive at least one mailing promoting the benefits of some natural compound for use in the treatment of ailments from dry skin to hair loss, and yes, for ADD too. Drs. Goldstein and Ingersoll note that the idea behind these natural remedies comes from the theories of orthomolecular psychiatry. Huh? This approach is based on treating mental disorders by providing an optimum environment for the mind through use of megavitamins and minerals. By providing increased doses of these compounds, it is thought that a variety of disorders can be improved.

Besides vitamin and mineral products, many distributors promote products containing elements found naturally in plants, including those with leaves (such as herbs and flowering plants) and those without leaves (coming from the algae and fungi families). Currently in my own mailbox are fliers for compounds such as blue-green algae, extract of tree bark, oil of primrose and various mineral/vitamin supplements, all suggesting relief from the effects of ADD. The literature accompanying these mailings boasts numerous success stories where the traditional prescription medications had either failed to provide any results, or had provoked side effects too prominent to live with.

These natural remedies, as I classify them, are said to minimize the effects of ADD. None that I have researched claim to cure ADD, although some distributors of the commercially available natural remedies do promise a lessening of effects over the years with continued use. According to a fact sheet provided by CHADD, some physicians may suggest natural remedies as part of an ADD treatment plan but most recommend the more traditional and tested methods of treatment, namely the combination of meds and accommodation.

A large number of parents on one particular Internet list that I peruse have reported that their children have responded well to the use of natural remedies. However, just as many or more, have reported that these remedies provided little or no relief from ADD effects. Further, some parents noted that the availability and cost of such remedies were obstacles to their consideration of using them.

Probably the most important factor to remember is to always, *always* check with your doctor before trying any remedy, whether its a mega-vitamin sold through a distributor, extracts from your nutritionist, or herbs grown in your own garden for medicinal use. Natural remedies come with their side effects, too. For example, excess doses of Vitamin D can lead to loss of appetite, weakness, depression and kidney trouble, to list a few. Too much Vitamin A can cause headaches, fatigue, and nausea. Too much Vitamin C can interfere with absorption of the B Vitamins.

Mineral supplements taken to extremes can cause side effects as well. Iron, in excess amounts can lead to liver damage! Too much zinc can interfere with the body's absorption of copper and iron resulting in abdominal pain, vomiting, and fatigue. Reported this year by the Associated Press (AP) in my town's daily newspaper, a "natural" herbal stimulant has been blamed for killing 15 people across the nation and causing hundreds more people dangerous side effects. You get the idea. Please check with a trusted physician or pharmacist before trying *any* product used for medicinal purposes, whether it's natural or something else.

Cure

A third outcome of ADD treatments might be listed as cure by some. *Treatments that attempt to cure are those that heal or get rid of an ailment.* Can you imagine? Not having to worry about ADD medicines and accommodation methods, reward charts, special diets, etc., and your child is eased of ADD's effects - for good? What a dream that is. Or is it a dream? There are those who insist that there are cures for ADD. In Chapter 2, I introduced methods of treatment including some that are offered as a cure, based on their premise of what causes ADD.

Symmetric Tonic Neck Reflex Therapy

The first such method comes from the theory that a leftover reflex from a child's crawling days is the culprit, and that if this reflex is worked through and eliminated, so will the effects of ADD perish as well. The symmetric tonic reflex develops between four and eight months of age and helps us as babies to extend our head and neck as we learn to crawl. Through about six months of crawling this reflex eventually matures and disappears, such as the sucking reflex disappears when we grow out of the infant stage.

Educators Dr. Nancy O' Dell and Dr. Mary Cook from the University of Indiana have continued research begun there over 25 years ago. This research shows that if a child does not crawl enough to ease this reflex from the body, the leftover reflex causes discomfort. This discomfort then translates into the traits exhibited in the ADD child of all types. Why would a child not crawl enough to lose this reflex? Drs. O'Dell and Cook say babies may be encouraged to walk more than crawl, babies may be placed into walkers too early (the kind where baby sits in but can lean against and "walk" around), babies may be confined to playpens and such, and so on.

If this theory of the leftover symmetric tonic reflex is indeed the trouble for our ADD kids, what do we do? Crawl? Yes, crawl. In their book, their teachings in college classes, and in their Treatment Center, these educators teach children to properly crawl and are given a recommended plan to continue crawling at home. Treatment efforts may involve at least fifteen minutes a day, five days a week, for about six months. Drs. O'Dell and Cook have their college students crawl too, as part of their grade! Says Cook, "If you don't have this leftover reflex plaguing you, you can't possibly know or feel the resulting discomfort or the effects it can cause." Students learn the method correctly by doing it themselves, perhaps gaining at least some compassion for the children they may someday treat.

This specific type of physical therapy has gotten flippant responses from the medical profession, but at the University of Indiana they are racking up the success stories. From an article in The Indianapolis Star, January 1, 1994, one mother claims that after the crawling sessions were taught and followed rigorously at home, her son's ADD effects improved so much that he now takes no meds, needs only minimal accommodation at school, and the ADD seems to be disappearing!

In an Indiana publication titled *Indy's Child* dated April 1987, O'Dell says that about 10% of the population is learning-disabled and of these, 75% may be helped through this method. She notes that while the exercises didn't solve all the children's difficulties, they did help the children to become more comfortable in school settings - writing became easier, attention spans increased and sitting was more comfortable. As reported in that article written by Susan Guyett, O'Dell says, "All I can say is that everybody who has ever finished the program as we've prescribed it has made significant improvement. In most cases grades go up. In every case work is accomplished more easily and in less time."

If your child is one (like mine) who crawled only for a short period of time or who spent a lot of time in a walker for example, check out this theory. Thanks to a new book by Drs. O'Dell and Cook (Avery Publishing Group, Inc. phone 1-800-548-5757) we too can try this fascinating method. It may not be the answer for all ADD sufferers; perhaps those who did crawl correctly as infants; but it seems harmless enough to try as long as you keep your child's total treatment plan unrestricted. Check the Resource Section for an address of the center where you write for more information.

Inner Ear Imbalance / CVS System

Dr. Levinson (See Chapter Two) promotes his treatment method as both a way to minimize effects and as a possible cure. His treatment as a cure can be realized if and when a patient sees a lessening of effects over time, eventually reaching a point of being ADD-free. This is reached, as we learned earlier, by a specific combination of medications to treat an imbalance in the inner ear. More specifically, he focuses on the cerebral vestibular system (CVS).

The cerebellum is part of the brain that controls coordination of voluntary movement. The vestibular system includes receivers found in the inner ear that respond to gravity and position, and movement of the head. Together this CVS system regulates energy levels, balance, speech and language, memory, moods and so on. Problems arise when an imbalance, whether naturally occurring or caused by illness, infection or injury, occurs in the CVS system, thus creating the characteristics of ADD and learning problems.

Dr. Levinson notes that while some patients will require some level of medication throughout adulthood, some can enjoy a shorter term period of treatment - a few years or so. For those who find success in just a few years, it would surely seem their cure has been found.

Time

Can time heal this ailment? The age-old and challenged assumption that ADD goes away in time may not be so farfetched after all - at least for some children. From a report issued by CHADD, consider these findings: *while the prevalence of ADD in adults is currently unknown, we do know that of the 3-5% of children who have ADD, about two-thirds of those diagnosed in or before elementary school continue to have symptoms in adolescence. And, one-third to one-half of these adolescents continue to have symptoms during their adult years.*

Hey! What about that one-third of the original 3-5 % of children diagnosed in or before elementary school who *don't* carry symptoms into adolescence? What about the other two-thirds to one-half of adolescents who *don't* have troublesome symptoms into adulthood? Whether they've been able to mature and work through their difficulties or whether the ADD just diminished, if it's gone is it cured? Time. Time may be moving slowly in your child's ADD cycle right now, but perhaps it is time that will indeed provide the cure - for some. Of course, what we do to help our children through these rough times is certainly as big a part of the cure - if we were to just let our children wait it out, the consequences of ADD's effects would undoubtedly cause lasting emotional, social and economic problems, long after these one-third "grow out" of their ADD.

Change the World

Imagine our children, being themselves. At their best and at their worst - could be the same. And the world embraces them, appreciates and encourages them. They are the "hot" blend of salsa, the "fluorescent" tone of paint, the complex equation. Our children. They go beyond the simple yet can see simply. They have passion for life, their energy internal as well as external.

The cure? Change the world. Create an atmosphere free of judgment. Advocate understanding. Champion acceptance. Sound like the pathway to world peace? Probably. Okay, so I was only dreaming, but it would *kind of* be a cure...

Back to reality and the real, judgmental, un-accepting, not very understanding world. Back to accommodation and minimizing effects. Our next chapter focuses on our children and their schools.

5

SCHOOL DAZE: WORKING THROUGH THE MAZE

When retailers begin advertising back-to-school sales, normally in the heat of July, they often portray reluctant, yet excited students and their relieved, rejoicing, peace-seeking parents.

However, many of us parents of ADD children do *not* see the beginning of school as a welcome break. We know that back-to-school means tremendous efforts helping our children readjust to the school day structure, new teachers, and new, higher expectations. We hold our breath, waiting for that first phone call or note from a frustrated teacher. We rack our brains, trying to figure out just what accommodation will be needed *this* year.

While indeed each new school year is an adventure all its own, there are measures to take, tips to try, skills to learn that can ease these efforts year after year. This chapter focuses on such skills and tips including: those that will help your child the student, those that will help you work with teachers (and other school assistants) toward effective strategies, those that help you work with school policy to get appropriate help for your child.

While I personally believe that the best and most useful efforts are those that focus on your child the student, I have chosen to begin discussing those strategies focusing on working with school policy. That way we can get the school rhetoric down to a language we understand and can refer back more easily to items that are related.

Working With School policy; Speak softly but carry a big stick

Most teachers and school administrators are very interested in providing whatever means are necessary to enhance learning and success for their students. However, there are times when, as parents, we must be loud and demanding concerning the services our children need. How do we know when to use the "big stick"?

An educational guide published by the Parent Education Network (PEN) said it well when it suggested, "When it is raining lightly... use the umbrella of your life long skill experiences. When it is pouring... use the umbrella of special guarantees under the Individuals with Disabilities Education Act - IDEA[Public Law (PL) 94-142, PL 99-457], section #504 of the Vocational Rehabilitation Act of 1973, and your state's special education standards and regulations." Just what are all these acts, provision, titles, etc.? Read on...

According to a report compiled by The National Information Center for Children and Youth with Disabilities (NICHCY), the IDEA and its amendments mandates minimum requirements for free appropriate public education of children and youth with disabilities, including early intervention services, and defines these children's rights. Each state then develops specific policies for special education and related services for children with disabilities in that state, using IDEA as a guideline. Each local public school district follows these guidelines and will base its policies on those federal laws and regulations, as well as on the laws and policies developed by the state.

Schools are required to provide parents copies of their state's special education and early intervention policies as requested. Those of you choosing private or parochial school, don't panic. Children's rights are guaranteed for your kids too, even if you choose a school where you must pay tuition.

Section 504 of the Rehabilitation Act of 1973 focuses on the factors of exclusion and discrimination. If a child with a disability is excluded from public education, from participation in, or denied the benefits of, or subjected to discrimination under any program or activity on the basis of his disability, then Section 504 applies.

Students with disabilities must have equal opportunity to participate in such things as non-academic services, extra-curricular activities, health services, recreational services, referrals to service providers, counseling services, etc. While it may seem that many of the services relate to physical disabilities, learning disabilities, including ADD, are covered as well. Think of Section 504 as a really, really big stick. Hopefully you'll never have to use it, but its there if need be. Section 504 also applies to secondary education as well. See the resource section for information on PEN and NICHCY.

Through the Maze

So, how do you decide if it's raining or pouring, and how do you get from "I think my child has a problem" to arriving at a plan that will provide appropriate, effective help? There are many steps that lead from suspecting a problem to the formal plan of action. Sometimes just following the steps along the way provide a vision of exactly the help that is needed. Sometimes it may seem that a formal plan is not quite enough.

Referring back to PEN's analogy, begin by using the umbrella of your lifelong skills. You are the one in your child's life who will follow her progress indefinitely. You are the one who can make the difference that he needs. Begin by using your intuitive skills. You have a unique feel for your exceptional child. Use it to begin finding the right path for her special needs, his optimum environment for learning.

Begin by scheduling a conference with your child's teacher. Do not use the regularly scheduled conference that normally occurs just after the first marking period ends. Those conferences are typically limited in time and are used to focus on a student's general performance. You will need at least thirty minutes to discuss your concerns and to gather the teacher's feedback. Strapped for time? Horrendous schedule? Send a note and ask for feedback in writing.

If at all possible make every effort to work with the teacher first, before charging into the principal's office or cornering a school board member at a social event. One school principal I know had a policy that she would listen to parents' concerns only after they had consulted with their child's teacher. Then, and only then she would agree to meet and have discussion. The idea is to work with the person closest to your child and his needs, then reach out to those who have increasing responsibility: teacher, remedial teacher, principal, school board member, etc.

Just as in the corporate world, schools have a chain of command as well. Recognize and use this chain of command appropriately. As long as your child attends a particular school system, your actions too will be associated with him, good and not-so-good. I'm not suggesting to be so gentle that you cannot get results; only to be appropriately firm. If you can't seem to figure out your school's chain of command, ask someone involved with a parent-teacher organization, or someone chairing a fund raiser - they'll know who's who.

After communicating and perhaps negotiating with your child's teacher and others, you may have come up with some effective strategies that will enhance learning and your child's success. If, on the other hand, you're all out of suggestions, it's probably time to follow the more formal route to possibly obtain special services.

NICHCY suggests these steps as an effective path to follow in your pursuit; the steps were designed to follow requirements of the IDEA.

First a referral or request for evaluation is made, either by parents or a professional (teacher, principal, psychologist). If a professional requests an evaluation, the school or service provider must notify the parents in writing.

Second is the evaluation itself. The initial evaluation can be conducted only with parental permission. The evaluation must assess the child in several areas, such as social and academic development, current level of performance versus potential, and so on.

Third, the results are reviewed by a team of school personnel, usually including a school psychologist, special education teachers, administrators, and others. Parents may be invited to attend this meeting. Eligibility for special services is normally determined at this meeting. Special services may include placement in a special education classroom or school, special enhanced opportunities in addition to regular classroom learning, individualized counseling, etc.

The fourth step includes two possibilities: A) If a child is found ineligible for special services, she would stay in her current placement, possibly along with remedial or other types of assistance and accommodation. B) If found ineligible, parents can disagree with the decision and have the right to take their child for an Independent Educational Evaluation (IEE) if they feel the initial evaluation was improperly done. The school must consider the results of am IEE.

-or-

Fifth, if your child is found eligible for special services, a meeting is planned at which the parents must be invited to attend. At this meeting, the child's Individualized Education Plan (IEP) is written. *An IEP includes goals and objectives of the child's program, types of special services that are needed, and amount of time the child will spend in regular educational activities.* Where the plan is to be implemented is another determination made at this meeting. Known as placement, this could be in a regular classroom with necessary support services, a resource room for a specified amount of time, a self contained class, or a separate facility. Parents have the right to agree or disagree with the IEP and its proposed placement.

Sixth, if there is disagreement, parents discuss any concerns about the IEP and move toward a compromise. Hopefully all concerns can be answered and the IEP adjusted reflecting those concerns. If appropriate effort has been made but a compromise cannot be reached, then parents can begin their Due Process Rights. This could involve further conferences with school officials, mediation services, hearings with school district officials and Office of Civil Rights representatives, and eventually civil action in court.

Seventh, the IEP and its placement must be reviewed at least once per year, although parents or school personnel can request a review at any time. At such a review, changes can be made and agreed or disagreed upon. As long as a student is receiving special services, the IEP and placement is reviewed at least every year, and an in-depth evaluation conducted at least every three years.

While the process tends to be somewhat confusing and some of the steps may seem unnecessary or duplicated, it is important that the procedures are followed fully. If you are ever faced with having to "use the system" in due process, you will have needed to fulfill the requirements of "exhausting all administrative procedures" which is legal talk for "following each and every step."

Now that we've learned about the rules and regulations, the processes and possibilities, and know where to refer back to their explanations, let's focus on your child's teacher.

Working With Your Child's Teacher; With or Without an IEP

Okay, so maybe it's a new school year or maybe it's a new school. If your child already has an IEP in place (remember that's an Individualized Education Plan) it will follow her to a new grade and to a new school as well. And, you have probably already met with the teacher prior to the start of school, as according to the IEP. But what if your child doesn't have a formal IEP? What if you have been able to implement effective strategies so far, or maybe your child's ADD effects are manageable enough not to warrant an IEP? Do you bring up the subject of your child's ADD, or not?

Do you spill the ADD beans, gently warning the teacher about your son's troubling behaviors; hopefully encouraging teacher to be aware of your daughter's academic challenges? Or, do you keep the information under your ADD hat for now, giving your child some time to accommodate herself, and having faith that the teacher will create an appropriate environment for her students?

It's probably a mix of both approaches. If you're totally up front, the ADD-ignorant (see Chapter 3) teacher may form, consciously or not, a negative judgment - dooming your child to failure for the semester. On the other hand, he may be knowledgeable about ADD and extra supportive in his teaching methods, so it would be to your child's advantage to discuss the ADD right away.

My suggestion? Give the new school year a bit of time to sink in, then decide how much or how little you need to share.

Harry, dad of eight-year-old Bradley, relates, "I knew that I had some breathing room, some time to assess Bradley's third grade situation, when the teacher sent a letter home to all parents. In it she explained how she believed each child to be a gift from God, each with his or her own strengths and challenges. She went on to map out her strategy to provide the best learning environment she could, depending on each child's gifts, with an open offer for suggestions and comments. I knew then that Bradley would be all right. She found ways to accommodate him that we still employ. As a matter of fact, it was his best school year, ever. It's not always that easy, though. In fourth grade, we got a call from the teacher the second week, asking us 'Is there a problem with Bradley?' Each year the situation requires a little different strategy."

On the other side of the issue sat Lydia's mom. This mom cautiously sent her first grader to school without explicit instructions to the teacher concerning her ADD challenges. Around the fourth week she knew she had to intervene - there were too many papers coming home with big red letters spelling out such negatives as "Sloppy", "Minus 10 (or whatever number was wrong)" and even a big fat "No!" Lydia needed positives like "Keep Trying", "2 Right", or "Improving." Fortunately Lydia hadn't become too frustrated at this point, and it was still early enough to make a change. Earlier intervention may have made things a bit easier, although it depends a lot on the teacher's style.

Another way to decide how and when to confer with teachers is to ask our children what *they* think, especially as students head into the fourth grades and beyond. These are the years when girls start calling their moms *"Mother,"* peer pressure has begun to escalate, and boys try to be independent but underneath they still feel like they need *their* mamas.

The years heading to adolescence is a time when you'll need to change your approach to your child's treatment plan. Think of it as a team effort - your child now makes many of his own decisions that you won't be able to directly affect. You can suggest, lead by example, etc. but you can't choose for him. So, why not begin by consulting him on this year's school strategy as well.

Requesting Teachers - Yay or Nay?

Each school has its own policy concerning placement of students with certain teachers. There may be some advantage in choosing one teacher over another; a certain teacher having more experience teaching exceptional students, for example. Or, choosing a particular placement to avoid possible conflict; bypassing a teacher who just doesn't "buy into" the realities of ADD and its effects on students.

Teacher choice may be part of the IEP, agreed upon by the administration, school staff, and the parents. Or you may be able to request a certain teacher simply by meeting with your school principal. One school district in my town requires a written petition that includes reasons for such a request.

Even if you can request teachers, should you make that choice? Marty ponders the question, "If I really personally knew the teachers in my daughter's school, maybe I would think about requesting one over another. But, I don't feel I can make that choice, so I trust the administration to do so on her behalf."

Mallory strongly believes in making teacher choices for her children. She says, "I have five kids in our school system, so I have gotten to know which teachers will mesh well with each of my kids' personalities. I make requests for all of them, ADD or not."

Finally, let's listen to the kids themselves. Suzi is a ten-year-old who has made it very clear that she doesn't want her *"mother"* creating a commotion at *her* school. "After four years of closely monitoring Suzi's educational program and progress, Suzi begged me to 'cool it', to let her handle things," says her mom. "That includes choosing teachers. She has come to resist the idea that she needs 'special' attention. She just wants to be like anyone else at this age, although she's like no one else! We try to let the system work as it's designed to and work to solve conflicts when they come up - and they do."

Focus On The Student

Some of the most effective strategies that can make a difference for your child are those that strive to understand and utilize her strengths. It makes sense, then, that school strategies focus on those strengths as well by learning to recognize students' particular learning styles, and by providing educational methods to fit them, both at school and at home. Where do we begin such a search for our child's strengths? We learn about the unique ways we learn.

Learning Styles

Unique is the basis for the theory of multiple intelligence, as suggested by Howard Gardner, psychologist and co-director of the Harvard Project on Human Potential. Dr. Gardner suggests that we possess not one, but seven unique forms of intelligence: Linguistic, Logical-Mathematical, Spatial, Bodily-Kinesthetic, Musical, Interpersonal, Intrapersonal. [Source: *Schooling at Home - Parents, Kids and Learning.* (J Muir Publications / Mothering Magazine)]

Within these seven forms of intelligence, some are stronger and some are weaker in each of us. This becomes so relevant for ADD children since schools, and the American society in general, typically reinforce only the linguistic (good with words) and logical-mathematical (good with logic) forms of intelligence. Many children are labeled learning disabled if their strengths are found, or ignored, outside these two forms of intelligence.

The seven forms, as noted by Gardner, are explained below. See if you can pinpoint your child's area of strength. Need help? Your school counselor can help uncover a student's sometimes hidden strengths - ask her! I've also listed some educational tools and activities that may enhance that particular intelligence. The idea is to adapt a usual learning activity so that it utilizes the child's strengths.

Linguistic - Learns through words (books, word processing, tape recorders, speaking and writing activities)

Logical-Mathematical - Learns through logical concepts (puzzles, strategy and detective games, brain teasers, science activities)

119

Spatial - Learns through images and visualization (charts, graphs, maps, art supplies, building supplies, visualization activities)

Bodily-Kinesthetic - Learns through tactile and bodily sensation (space to move, gyms, modeling clay, sports equipment, video computer games)

Musical - Learns through sounds, melody and rhythm (percussion and other musical instruments, records and tapes, computer sound systems, things to tap and strum on)

Interpersonal - Learns through social interaction (clubs, committees, group work, after school activities, peer teaching)

Intrapersonal - Learns through self study and awareness (Self paced instruction, solo games and sports, quiet retreat spots, journals and diaries, self-esteem activities)

Now let's use the activity of studying spelling words and adapt the lesson to each learning style*:

Learning Style:	Adapted Lesson:
Linguistic	Use the computer to make a list of words. Use each word in a sentence to create a story.
Logical-Mathematical	Create a word search using the spelling words. Design a crossword puzzle with the words.

Spatial	Write the spelling words in the air. Look at the word, spell it aloud with eyes closed, see it in your mind.
Bodily-Kinesthetic	Create letters out of clay or dough to spell the words. Trace the words with your finger in a tray filled with sand. Use your body to shape each letter of the word.
Musical	Sing the spelling of each word to a familiar tune. Tap out a rhythm for each letter. Make up a song using the words. Make a tape recording of the words to a beat or to music.
Interpersonal	Invite a friend over to study. Call a friend and quiz each other. Start a study club that meets each week before test day.
Intrapersonal	Create a quiet, comfortable retreat with room for one. Write words in a special journal. Tape record yourself spelling the words then listen on a set of headphones.

*At the end of each adapted spelling lesson the student should write the words with pencil and paper as well, if that's how the test will be given at school; that is unless part of your child's accommodation plan includes taking tests in his most successful way.

Gardner Knows Our Geniuses

All children, apart from those suffering severe brain damage, have unlimited potential for intelligence, according to Gardner. We all possess all seven forms of intelligence. Some of us are well rounded in all areas while some of us have a natural strength in just one particular area or two and almost no ability in others. By utilizing our strengths to learn and grow, we can enhance our total level of intelligence. Gardner believes that no one type of intelligence should be given priority (such as the importance of words and logic in school), as they all are equally important.

He concludes that considering this multiple intelligence theory, every child quite possibly has the potential to be a genius in at least one of the areas of intelligence. Then, we already knew that about our extraordinary children!

Tips and Skills for School Days

In this section you'll find a variety of tips for the school environment that can easily be adapted for home. These words of wisdom come from a multitude of sources, some well known and some unknown. I've perused and picked and organized these tips into categories. Sources include ADD researchers, therapists, doctors, authors, teachers, support groups and parents: C. Anderson, R. Barkley, L. Braswell, D. Brooks, CHADD, L. Clark, P. Collonna, P. Cook, C. Cunningham, A. Fehr, M. Fowler, H. Ginott, S. Goldstein, M. Gordan, E. Gray Gorr, B. Ingersoll, T. Hartmann, E. Kosh, J. Miller, A. Miller,

H. Parker, S. Reif, S. Wagaman, S. Zentall, etc. Try one, try them all!

To Help Sustain Attention

- Move around the room while teaching
- Develop cues like a tap on the shoulder, eye contact, or private signals to help student stay on task
- Break assignments into smaller parts (chunking)
- Ask student to repeat directions
- Reduce quantity of work but require quality
- Provide testing breaks; time to stretch or walk around
- Alternate high and low interest activities
- Provide peer tutors
- Use partners, small groups, or centers
- Shorten or divide work periods and use a timer to end
- Allow child to sit close to teacher
- Use overhead projector
- Highlight directions on papers and operational signs in math
- Teach student how to highlight his own work
- Provide a proofreading or editing checklist for student to use
- Avoid multiple commands
- Provide small, frequent social or material awards (points, stars, applause, etc.)

To Help Stay on Task

- Allow student to take tests away from class, in a resource room for example, away from distractions.
- Arrange classroom with separate space for each desk
- Surround a child with good role models

- Place child's desk away from distractions (window, door, heater, fish tank)
- Play softly near the student a tape recording of beeps placed at certain time intervals (2-3 minutes) for self monitoring

To Keep Extra Energy Under Control
- Use activity as a reward (run errands, erase blackboards)
- Allow standing during seatwork
- Provide busywork activities when work is completed (sorting clips, folding papers)
- Permit student to handle *small* objects that are kept in desk when sustained attention is required (pipe cleaner, twist tie)
- Allow moving around in classroom if not disruptive
- Ignore unwanted behavior which is not disruptive
- Praise times when student returns to task on his own

To Curb Impulsivity
- Advise child in advance about upcoming activities when self control will be necessary
- Call on student only when she is paying attention or has hand raised
- Ignore child's calling out without raising hand
- Praise child when hand is raised
- Teach child how to self monitor. Child asks herself, "Did I call out? Did I raise my hand?", then notes on a card with +/−.

Aiding Organization
- Use color coded folders and notebooks
- Have a predictable, consistent schedule
- Post schedule in class and tape to student's notebook
- Provide an extra set of textbooks for home use
- Schedule weekly desk organization for entire class

- Provide assignment book and model its use
- Write assignments and test dates on board to be recorded in assignment book
- Write key words or outline on board during lecture
- Allocate a time at day's end to record assignments and due dates, gather books and materials
- Allow student to seek assistance from others
- Set up a "homework partner" that each student can call on at home for unrecorded, mis-recorded assignments
- Designate one teacher as coordinator if multiple teachers

Ease Into Transitions
- Inform student of any changes in the normal routine ahead of time
- Provide supervision during transition time (lunch, recess, class change, dismissal)
- Have consistent rules and expectations in all settings (class, assembly, lunch, art)
- Have consistent rewards, grades, consequences, written directions etc. if child has more than one teacher

To Enhance Memory
- Organize desk and locker with labels
- Tape reminder cards to desk, books, folders
- Ask student to repeat directions
- Provide both oral and written directions
- Establish routines (have tests on same day each week)
- Teach entire class how to use calendar and assignment book

Tuning Fine Motor Skills
- Do not require student to recopy materials
- Allow use of computer, tape recorder

- Permit printing or lower expectations for acceptable writing
- Allow extra time for copying assignments or completing tests or worksheets
- Allow oral test for essay questions
- Accept homework done on computer
- Permit classmates to share notes copied on machine
- Use multiple choice, matching, true/false tests (minimal writing)

Encourage the Positive & Build Self Esteem
- Post rules prominently in class
- State rules positively ("Walk" *not* "Don't Run")
- Enforce rules immediately
- Avoid argument or confrontation by using private cue to signal the need for time out in a quiet location
- Teach social skills by role playing good models of behavior
- Teach students calming strategies (counting to ten, slow breathing)
- Solicit student input to handle conflict
- Employ peer mediation activities (a group of student helpers)
- Ignore daydreaming which does not disrupt others
- Use encouraging statements on low quality work ("Keep Trying", "Improving", "You're Coming Along")
- Avoid comparing students to others
- Tell them what you like that they did
- Do not permit humiliation, teasing or scapegoating by peers
- Praise in public, Reprimand in private
- Reduce competitive activities in class
- Mark correct responses, not number of errors
- Incorporate children's interests and hobbies into lessons

Good Communications

- Create a method to easily communicate with parents/teachers (A home-to-school folder; weekly for older students, daily for younger students)
- Designate one teacher as liaison if there are more than one
- Teachers, ask parents what works well at home
- Parents, ask teachers what works well at school
- Make positive phone calls or write "good things" notes to share improvements and successes
- For younger children. Use a simple chart with happy, neutral, or sad faces to indicate what kind of day child had or for tracking goals (walk in lunch line)
- For older children, use plus, check, or minus on a weekly basis
- Call or write for pre-determined reasons (drop in grades, inappropriate behavior)

Managing Medication

- Have the school nurse or other adult designated by the principal administer the medication (*other* than teacher and *away* from the classroom))
- Privately cue student when it is time to take medication
- Make sure directions to administer medication are clearly stated from physician
- Have a plan for when child needs to take medicine away from school (field trip, etc.)

Ask Your School To Try These

- Provide in-service training on ADD
- Alert other school staff (secretaries, bus drivers, cafeteria workers) to student needs, with parent permission

- Post written copy of public address announcements
- Provide public recognition of students' accomplishments
- Adjust class scheduling (difficult in morning, specials in afternoon)
- Establish a consistent use of assignment books across grades
- Develop school wide standard headings on tests, worksheets
- Provide information to parents on groups such as CHADD, NICHCY, etc.
- Create support groups for parents with like concerns
- Create in school support groups for students with like needs

Homework Help

Certainly use the previous tips and skills for home use as well. Just adapt them to your home environment. Here are some additional ideas to consider that focus on how kids "work" at home.

When preparing kids for homework duty, many educators propose using the consistency theory - homework is done at the same time, same place, same pace each week day. Scheduling homework in such a manner certainly may work well for some students. However, using consistency too rigidly can turn homework time into the battle zone for others.

Providing flexibility when needed and knowing what works best for your child is key. ADD-mom Sandy notes, "Some days my son wants to take care of his studies right away, and some days he needs to "let loose" before settling down to work. On those days, we agree to a time frame when he feels calm enough to benefit from his studies."

Another way to handle the homework situation is to break it up into bits. Many times the amount of homework required on a particular evening may seem like a mountain to a child with attention challenges. Doing a little at a time may help ease her frustration. Yes, it takes more effort and time to complete studies this way, but a child's self esteem and your sanity are far more important than getting homework done in one sitting. Rosie is such a student. Her dad shares their homework technique. "If it's Scout or gymnastics night, my daughter may choose to tackle her homework in pieces, some before and some after activities. I used to insist she get it all accomplished before heading out to activities, but I found that she did better work without having to rush. On a 'quiet' evening, she spreads her homework out, sometimes taking all night to complete it, but then, it is normally well done."

What about the child who sits and stares at homework, crying for yet another break or trip to the bathroom? You can begin to develop a stick-to-it ability by encouraging your child to try to continue for just a couple more minutes when he seems ready to flee. Using a timer to count stick-to-it time and break time can help keep you out of the time-keeper role, and into the role of supporter. Try using encouraging remarks such as, "Wow! You've got three questions finished already. Keep up the good work." And, don't forget to dole out the positive rewards (a hug, stickers, points, etc.) when he does manage to continue.

Some experts insist that parents offer a quiet place to study - a desk in the child's room or in a home office, for example. That may seem like logical advice for a child who easily becomes distracted, yet quiet alone doesn't guarantee she'll stay on task. Homework at my house does not typically get done in the quiet of the kids' rooms even if they're all alone. You already know how that works out for most ADD kids - you return thirty minutes later and there they sit, homework untouched.

Many musically oriented children, for example, work better if they can listen to soft music while studying. Some students find that the kitchen table is the place that helps them produce their best work. This is often a trait of the social/group learner. And what about the solo learner? One mother told me she often finds her daughter behind closed doors on the bathroom floor - working intently and humming to herself. Another confesses that her son usually does his best studying sitting on his basketball in the garage! Perhaps a kinesthetic student, that one.

Of course, as parents we need to teach our ADD children to be accountable for their school work. We can help by having the necessary homework tools available (pencils, paper, dictionary, stapler, crayons, etc.), suggesting an appropriate time and place for studies and coming to agreements on it all. Allowing a child to watch television all evening, then expecting him to scramble before bedtime to complete school assignments probably isn't the best way to teach a child how to set priorities. In any case, help your child find a place, time and pace that truly promotes focus on her work, and pour on the encouragement.

Other Learning Disabilities

While ADD is indeed a medical disorder, the strides made, such as assistance under federal programs that we reviewed earlier in this chapter, have been possible mostly due to ADD being classified as a learning disability. One question we ask ourselves when trying to diagnose our child's problem is most often, "Is the ADD causing these learning disabilities or is a learning disability causing frustrations that look like ADD?" In Chapter 2 we discussed indicators that distinguish ADD behaviors from behaviors stemming from other learning disabilities, including the factors of how long and how often such behaviors occur. (See Chapter 2, *What is ADD?*) Many ADD children are also challenged by other learning disabilities. While it is estimated that about 3% of all children have learning disabilities, it has been found that about 35% of ADD children also have other learning disabilities. What are the other learning disabilities?

In the last 10 to 15 years, research has moved past the labeling of learning disabilities and has instead moved to describing *skill areas*, according to the National Institutes of Health (NIH). You may have heard terms such as dyslexia, which is many times perceived as a problem with transposing letters but is actually a term previously given to label any reading difficulty. The move toward describing skills that are deficient is aimed at understanding how to overcome the problem area.

From the article How to Spot A Learning Disability by Janet Bailey printed in *Working Mother*, January 1997, types of learning disabilities are described as:

• *Reading:* a deficit in this area may affect basic skills such as recognizing words and comprehension.

• *Writing:* a deficit in this area show up as a difficulty forming words, spelling or organizing ideas.

• *Listening:* a deficit in this area includes problems in discriminating between sounds, in recognizing units of sound that make up words, in understanding other people's speech when trying to follow directions.

• *Speaking:* a deficit in this area may affect the ability to find the right words to express an idea or to put words in the right order.

• *Mathematics:* a deficit in this area may cause problems with basic skills such as adding and multiplying as well as mathematical reasoning.

ADD's label was not replaced with a "skill area" but was listed in this article as a side note with the description "ADHD and its variants". Perhaps ADD's skill area could be listed as *attention* or *self-control.* If you notice any of the following, run, don't walk to your child's teacher for assistance.

EARLY WARNING SIGNS OF LEARNING DISABILITIES

The National Center for Learning Disabilities, a nonprofit national organization in NY, stresses that early detection and intervention is the best strategy, although they point out that people with learning disabilities can be helped at any age. Some of the early warning signs, according to this group, include:

- Rhyming difficulties, the most frequent predictor of reading problems.

- Problems with: learning letters, pronouncing words, understanding questions, writing, following directions, explaining things.

- Memory problems such as reciting the alphabet, remembering names and events, learning new tasks.

- Organization and attention difficulties; finishing tasks, concentrating, finding belongings.

The Center points out that no child is perfect at these skills all the time, but that if problems consistently show up in more than one, an expert should be consulted.

The National Center for Learning Disabilities can assist with information on local support groups in your area, call (212) 545-7510

(Source: How to Spot A Learning Disability by Janet Bailey printed in *Working Mother,* January 1997)

6

AFTER-SCHOOL SUCCESS

Time for some fun! Our kids work so hard, they deserve a break. Yet, finding the right activities for our children isn't as easy as just picking a class from a schedule. First, we need to consider the reasons or motives for enrolling children in activities. Here are some reasons - you may have others: to have something the youngster can excel in, social interaction, physical activity, to enhance strengths, to build areas of weakness, to give the caretaker a break, learn a new skill, just for fun. So instead of rushing to sign up for the first soccer league you find, pause and reflect on why you're adding an activity to your child's schedule, and yours!

Your Child's Most Excellent Activity

One of the first pieces of advice I was given from a psychologist who focused on ADD patients, was to find some activity that my kids excelled in and let them excel. That advice is everlasting because it focuses on the good things a child has to offer, at any age. And, the opportunity to excel gives a child extra confidence to handle other areas of her life where there is most probably a struggle. Danny struggled with school subjects. He was slower picking up reading skills and so, other subjects suffered as well. But on the baseball diamond he was top notch. Coaches asked him to play in the Mustang league (a step up from tee ball and one step below Pony) when he was just six years old. Although there were times when his attention level wasn't what it should have been, for the most part his love of the game helped him to curb his distractibility, at least on the field. Danny knew that while some kids were reading far above his own ability, they couldn't come close to his ability at bat or on first base, and that seemed to ease his frustration somehow. It helped too, that the children enjoyed an environment where their teacher placed high value on her students' individual gifts. Finding and celebrating our children's special talents can make a difference. Let them excel!

Social Interaction

Many of our ADD children struggle with applying appropriate social behavior. Whether their impulsive nature is knocking them out of grace or their inattentiveness to their peers is perceived as uncaring, there are activities that can help hone appropriate social behaviors. Organized activities such as scouts, 4-H, youth clubs, etc. are normally structured so that the children are expected to be part of and contribute to the group. The after school program certified by the YMCA has a built in social practice scheme; for twenty minutes at some point in the schedule all students are asked (required actually) to join in a special activity designed to develop social skills. It could be a game of charades, a relay race, a story telling chain, and so on. At the end of the activity, leaders take time to discuss any problems that came up during the event like poor sportsmanship. There are other model programs that focus on the child both as an individual and as a member of a group. Most scout programs, for example, start around the first grade, earlier for the girls' groups, and are designed to have several adult helpers that can act as role models for appropriate behavior. When looking for such a group, try to meet the leaders beforehand to gauge their personality match with your child's. Or, become a leader yourself if possible; unless of course one of your reasons for extra-curricular activities is:

To Give The Caretaker A Break

Don't feel guilty - sometimes enrolling your child in an activity is one of the only chances you get to take a breather. Sandy, parent of seven-year-old Andy agrees. She says, "Some of the only chances I get to be by myself are when Andy has a youth group meeting at our local YMCA. Sure, I have a single-parent group that I attend weekly, but the hour that I spend waiting for him while he's at his group can be very refreshing. Sometimes I walk on the indoor track. Sometimes I find a quiet corner to read or write in a journal I keep. Sometimes I just sit and watch the people go by. Yes, there are benefits for Andy, too; he gets to burn off energy in the gym or make a craft, and there's social interaction. But, I find his group time is time I don't want to give up!"

Physical Activity

A previous discussion concerning physical therapies as a way to ease effects of ADD (Chapter 4), suggested providing plenty of physical activity whether it is structured to "cure" ADD or serves as just an outlet for excess energy. On the one hand, many parents remark that after a rousing hour-and-a half soccer practice, their kids are "worn out." "Funny", says one ADD Dad, "My kid only seems to get more stimulated!" So, while kids can and do feel better about themselves after all kinds of physical activity, some kids' energy levels just seem to rise after such exertion. For those who do "burn out", using up that extra energy may be a welcome break for some parents.

For those whose ADD kids are fueled by that extra activity, well, just have a back-up plan ready to funnel that vitality. Physical activity is just as and perhaps more important for the inactive ADD child. Many times this child does not care to join in the action. Find some form of physical activity that suits, perhaps taking a walk outside or stretching to relaxing music.

To Build Areas of Weakness

Think of a skill your child needs to improve, then find or create an activity that provides skill practice while at the same time is entertaining. Laura tells about her efforts to find some interesting way to help her daughter Nicole improve her reading. "When summer school vacation rolled around I just couldn't see us hitting the same old tutoring route that we'd been used to. Although the tutors had been wonderful and the plan fairly effective, Nicole needed something new. I noticed on our church bulletin board that volunteer help was needed in a local pre-school program. Nicole responded and was accepted. Her job - to choose and read stories to the children, then encourage them to talk about what they'd heard. Nicole spent lots of time at our library choosing just the right books. She would read the books over and over until she felt confident with the words and her oral expression. She thought about what she had read - improving her comprehension level tremendously. It was a great experience and it did get her to read, a lot. She still finds time to read to the children, although not as much when school is in session."

To Enhance A Strength

Think back to Levinson's discussion about the 50/50 rule- at least 50% of our comments should be focused on positives. Likewise, when we think about extracurricular activities for our kids, consider something that your child can already do to some extent, then encourage him to strive toward higher attainment in that skill. For example, Jenna began playing the flute in the fourth grade and she liked playing an instrument. She had one, fifteen-minute lesson per week during school hours, and she often practiced at home. Jenna's mother suggested that she take more extensive lessons from a private music teacher, and Jenna was thrilled! After much practice, she was asked to play in the school band and in a select group formed by her private music teacher. Building upon a child's strengths can be one way to find an activity that matches her interests while providing success that positively affects other concerns (Jenna chose to complete a historical report on the origin of the flute for a school assignment). On the other hand, be careful not to insist that a child engage in an activity because *you* think he likes or is good at it. Take the music lesson scenario and insert the parent who assumes the child loves the clarinet and invests in top of the line private lessons, only to find out that the child joined the music program just to be excused from twenty minutes of class once per week!

Learn A New Skill

In the discussion about learning styles in the last chapter, we began trying to figure out just which style is most like our particular child. Sometimes the clues don't appear too readily and we have to pay very close attention to find them. Finding the right activities for our child can sometimes be a similar feat. Try some short-term activities that focus on learning a new skill. It could be a one time craft seminar or a four-week storytelling event. Many times our children's talents lay hidden until we find an outlet where they can shine. If your child is anxious about something so new, take a class together, or offer to assist in a session that is for kids only. Lots of choices can be found around the holidays especially, like crafts and other creative classes. Summer is also a popular time for short-term events to try something new. Local colleges, schools, and day-care centers offer such classes focusing on learning new skills: computers, sculpture, painting, swimming, sports, woodworking, foreign languages, etc. If your child finds something he really enjoys and wants to continue, simply ask the instructor for ideas on where to find more of the same!

Just For Fun!

One of the best remarks I ever heard from a parent picking up a child from an activity was this, "Did you have fun?" Some of the worst remarks I've heard: "Did you win?", "Gees, what took you guys so long?", "Come on let's get outta here!" "I'm glad *that's* over", "How many more times do we have to do to this?" Ouch. You can only imagine how a child receives such words. I have tried to replace my own less than encouraging remarks with that one gem, although I have been seen rushing down the halls of the YMCA, kids in tow panting. "Uh...Did you... have... fuuuuun?"

We've been talking about reasons for choosing one activity over another to match the interests and skills of our challenging kids. However, especially in their childhood, let's try to place the emphasis on fun! Kelli was reminded of this "fun focus" the day her son Jamie vowed to put away his karate uniform forever. At six years old Jaime was full of energy and loved the high kicking and jumping that the sport required. But the fun faded when Jaime was invited to join an advanced class based on his potential. Here he was expected to perform flawlessly and with great amounts of self-control. Though he had the physical maturity for the advanced class, he ended up in a time out corner at least once during every session for little annoying habits (chattering, tapping his feet, humming, etc.) So, when Jaime announced, "No, Mom, I never have fun here anymore", he was moved back to a class where he could. Take note!

After-School At Home

Not all after school activities need to be enjoyed away from home. One of the most beneficial things for some ADD kids is "down time." This phrase, coined by the computer industry meaning time the user had to spend waiting for the computer to re-set itself, makes great sense in our busy lives, too. It might take your family a few tries to strike the right balance of activities and down-time. Probably both are needed.

Michelle, a single mother of two boys, one ADD, agrees. "When I seemed to be spending more and more time yelling at the kids to 'find something to do', that's when I went full force and found them some activities away from home. Oh, we found judo, gymnastics, swimming, tee-ball, biddy basketball, art classes. But after about a year of running to this team and that practice every night and really finding no peace in it all, we stopped for a couple of months. Of course, then we were headed right back into the old 'there's nothing to do' trap again. Finally we settled on a scouting program which the boys just love, plus one team sport depending on the season. No overlapping baseball with soccer or judo with swimming. Soon the boys began to enjoy their time at home with 'nothing to do.' Sure, they still need some suggestions from time to time, but on the whole they find things to do during their down-time."

There are some fantastic books outlining fun activities to do at home, so I won't go deeper into those here. What I can offer is a way to lessen some (not all) of that sibling rivalry that seems to pop up whenever a game involves a bit of competition:

Time To Play The Cooperative Way

"What? Cooperation in my house? At play time? Everyone wins? No fighting?" Yep. Cooperative play can be a great way for kids to enjoy activities while building respect and harmony with playmates and siblings. It's a method of play where all players win if a goal is reached. Everyone works toward the same goal or encourages individual players to improve on their own performance. The idea of cooperative play is one subject from a huge volume titled *Helping Your Hyperactive Child* by John F. Taylor, Ph.D. (Prima Publishing & Communications.)

In cooperative checkers, for example, players try to move the black and red checkers to opposite sides of the board, one move at a time, with no checkers taken off the board and no moving backwards. Try cooperative drawing; each player makes a pencil or crayon stroke on his turn, adding a bit to the drawing without talking. The picture evolves from the cooperative spirit and creativity of the players. In cooperative *Scrabble ™*, players work as a team to make as many words as they can using up all the letters. Transform your favorite game into a cooperative one - keep a record of bowling scores; next time you hit the lanes each player tries only to beat her own last score, not everyone else's.

Cooperative play can improve interpersonal skills (getting along with others) by lessening resentment toward others' errors or ineffective performance. And, a person's outstanding ability becomes seen as an asset to the entire group. Also, less quarreling about cheating, lying, not knowing how to play, showing off, etc. certainly helps in any situation!

Sure, competition is a given in our society and we all need to learn to compete effectively. Our kids compete everyday, though, and cooperative play is a nice change.

"Mom (or Dad) Will You Play With Me?"

Doesn't it seem that just as we turn our efforts to supper, the bills, the laundry, etc. a little voice comes to us, begging for our time. And, we know the right thing to do, don't we? Hundreds of self-help books have warned us to "leave the dirt, love the child" or some other clever saying that usually only leaves us feeling guilty for the choices made. Granted, you just can't play all day. Parents have to get things done. If we let our kids run around in ragged clothing or allow them to live in a home with mounds of clutter laying around, we'd be suspected of endangering their welfare!

However, it is possible to take time to play with our children while taking care of the other responsibilities that do have to get finished. It's all in the timing. Next time your child begs, "Mom (or Dad) can you play with me?" and you've truly got to finish a task that must be done, try this solution - set a time limit, maybe 10 - 15 minutes that you can devote to your child right now or at a specified time not too much later. Let her choose an activity and abide by her rules. Knowing that the deal will be done in a certain time frame might make you more agreeable to stop what you're doing at the moment and play. John had this to say about taking bits of time with his son, "Many times I find that the time we've spent goes well beyond the initial ten minutes or so, and then I get back to whatever it was that was so pressing." My daughter typically wants to play Monopoly (the real one, not the Jr. edition) and you know what a time beast that can be. She has it set up in the basement and we play for our specified time, to be continued another time, if that's her choice.

Some parents have responded that if their kids can count on these snippets of time, they are more apt to enjoy the time, then find something to do on their own. It's not a quantity

versus quality time issue. My personal feeling is that quantity
time is also necessary! But, for the times when you really must
turn to other responsibilities, these short term activities can get
you through until you can spend more time. And don't forget,
in turn you get time for activities of your choice.

7

A LIFETIME OF APPROPRIATE BEHAVIOR

Who's Who in Behavior Expertise

Throughout previous chapters we've discussed in part some of the currently popular discipline approaches based on assertiveness, positive language, reward systems and so on. While researching the multitudes of information on discipline and behavior, the name of Dr. Haim G. Ginott continually appeared in references and as the basis of many titles. Dr. Ginott, now deceased, was a popular child expert in the 1960's. The librarian in my town told me she once heard him speak in Hershey PA, and that parents everywhere just loved him and his caring style. She said that he did not scold or judge in his lectures; he simply talked about children as the young people they are, and the needs that they have. Ginott in his popular title, *Between Parent and Child* (Macmillan Co. 1965), suggested not a discipline plan but rather a philosophy to prepare children for a lifetime of responsible, appropriate behavior. Many have adapted his ideas to current day thought.

Another popular pediatrician/author who originally earned fame for his 1946 book, *Baby And Child Care* is Dr. Benjamin Spock. Fifty years later, the book is in its sixth rendition with much of the original advice intact but with new twists designed to take parents into the 21st century. In an

Associated Press release, Spock, who turned 93 in May of '96, said of his book, " The secret of its original success and its continued success was that is was kind to parents. There is a tendency on the part of professional people in medicine and psychology…to scold parents." Don't you just love *that* perception! He continued, "I was acutely aware that parents in America are easily made guilty and the best service I could perform was to tell them," 'You know more than you think you do.'"

So, for the balance of this chapter I have taken from Dr. Ginott, his followers, and a multitude of others to present an array of approaches to teaching your ADD child about responsible, appropriate behavior, for life. And, you won't be scolded!

What Exactly Makes Up A Lifetime of Appropriate Behavior?

When we talk about teaching or preparing our children for a "lifetime of appropriate behavior" it includes instilling responsibility and independence, setting limits and expectations, encouraging relationships, and implementing discipline when necessary. But perhaps the most important piece is communication.

Wait! Don't throw the book down just yet. You've been to parenting communications seminars that presented the correct phrases to use - *"How do you feel about that?"*. You've been encouraged to try *mirroring - a method where the listener repeats in a similar way what the speaker just said to check for meaning.* Me too. Not all of us can sincerely follow the programs, or perhaps we know what to do, it's just that we just don't do it. When I mention communication, I go back to Spock's previous quote that "you know more than you think you do." So, be yourself, trust yourself, and just...talk with your child.

Communicating

Talking *with* your child is a lot different than talking *to* your child. Talking with your child means you're not issuing orders or using language she doesn't understand. It means giving your child your undivided attention - maintaining eye contact, setting down the newspaper, listening, close physical proximity, and so on. Now, we cannot always stop what we're doing, but when it's important, or when it's necessary we must try. Our children need and should be able to count on us, on our one-to-one attention. Our ADD kids seem to count on our attention all of the time, I know. Use that intuition you have honed through this whole ADD experience to consider if *this* is a time for you to stop, look and listen, or if perhaps it is a time to just chat while you go on about your business. Hey, there are no perfect solutions, just lots of choices.

Besides talking and listening one-on-one whenever you can, try the advice of many communications experts - listen without judgment. Save your opinion until you're asked for it. Sometimes kids just need us to *sit there and shut-up and listen*. Sure, throw in an occasional "uh-huh", "I see", or nod every now and then - to show your interest. Then, try not to speak until your child seems to be finished or asks you a question with a pause. Then add a pause of your own before you speak. "Often, my ten-year-old daughter tells me about some dilemma she has," says Tom. "She asks questions that she really doesn't want me to answer. I've learned to wait to answer her because she often comes up with a solution to her problem on her own. I just hope she keeps talking to me through her teen years! I've tried to show that she can - without getting a lecture in return."

We could all try harder at improving our listening skills. For a start, try listening in a quieter way - without speaking! I often have to bite my lip or physically cover my mouth!

What about listening for meaning? Saint Francis of Assisi was one of the first on record to offer the idea of seeking understanding rather than the desire to be understood. In the nineties, Stephen Covey cornered the market on the popular phrase "Seek first to understand, then to be understood." The idea of being understood sounds quite pleasing to us as parents, for sure. Yet, it takes practice to try to understand first. This idea is yet another important part of communicating. When your child is speaking to you, do you sometimes cut him off, finish his sentence, assume you know exactly what he means?

Trying to understand is a gift you give, and it can save you from igniting an argument. Margie tells how a misunderstanding on her part ended in unwelcome silence. "Well, Maddie was going on and on about some jacket she just had to have. She's just so seldom satisfied. Anyway, I had had enough and began to remind her of all her things hanging in the closet. Finally she yelled at me, 'Mom you never listen to me!' and then locked herself in her room. Now at nine years old you wouldn't think that a jacket would mean so much. Well, I blew it and tried talking to her again but she had no time for me. Later I was chatting with my sister, recounting the whole scene when she reminded me that nine years old is a tough time socially, especially for girls. She said 'Maddie is probably just trying to feel her way around the circle.' The solution wasn't to cave in and promise her the jacket, but listening to her until she ran out of steam would have been a better choice. Maybe she would have gotten to her real concerns."

You can find your own phrases and techniques to communicate effectively. Just keep in mind the key points: make time to listen one-on-one, talk with not to your child, do more listening than talking, try to be non-judgmental, and listen first to understand. I have faith that you can do this without the canned phrases and formal mirroring techniques.

EFFECTIVE COMMUNICATING

- **Make Time to Listen One on One**
- **Talk *With* your Child, Not *To* your Child**
- **Do More Listening and Less Talking**
- **Be Non-Judgmental**
- **Listen First to Understand**

Responsibility

Some of the most challenging lessons to strive to teach our kids are those based on and focusing on responsibility. Challenging because, after all, our ADD kids are forever forgetful, rarely prepared, and more likely to be *irresponsible*. However, developing a responsible attitude can be encouraged. It's not often accomplished with negative punishment or pressure, but by modeling responsible behavior ourselves, and through noticing and commending kids' responsible behavior when it does occur. And, it will! So, when she comes in for dinner on time, and you say to her, "Janie, your being on time shows responsibility," she'll think to herself , "Oh, so that's what it means, that's what it feels like to be responsible."

Ginott points out that responsibility cannot be taught, imposed, or enforced. Responsibility in his terms does not mean raking the leaves or washing the dishes. He notes, " Insistence on performing chores may result in obedience and cleaner kitchens and yards, but it may have undesirable influence on the molding of character." Chores shouldn't be done just because "Mother said so." They should be done because it is something that needs to be done to keep the family home safe and organized, for example. Others, too echo this theme. Evonne Weinhaus and Karen Friedman, authors of *Stop Struggling With Your Child* (Harper Perennial 1991), devote an entire section to encouraging responsibility from within.

From a wealth of sources the idea remains, and I choose to agree, that responsibility grows from within and is stimulated by the values of the home and the community. Am I hinting that we are to blame for lack of responsibility in our kids? Not exactly. I promised, no scolding. It's more of an awareness of the responsible behavior we show or don't, and that which we choose to praise or ignore. It is based on our values. If our values are based on respecting others, taking care of those who can't, freedom, happiness, and honesty for example, then inner responsibility grows from that base. So, *I feed the dog because dad told me to* becomes *I feed the dog because he can't do it for himself and he'll get sick without a proper diet.*

On the other hand, if our values are based on negatives such as: everyone for himself, there's not enough for everyone, defend yourself, cheat to get ahead, etc., well then that responsibility can lead to destruction and anti-social behaviors. So, *I feed the dog because Dad told me to* becomes *Let someone else do it, I'm busy.*

Even if our values are the base for building responsible behavior, we tend to notice those *things* left undone or the *actions* that are lacking as a measure of our child's level of responsibility. Things like unfinished homework, messy rooms, un-fed pets and so on are not necessarily clues of an irresponsible child. In the larger sense, it is a path to follow, not a thing forgotten or action ignored. A child may be well-mannered, tidy and academically graced, and yet can still act irresponsibly.

A mother wrote to a syndicated advice columnist in her local newspaper. She wondered how she could make her daughters more responsible for the state of the room they shared. It was the messiest room ever, she claimed - just disgusting! Dirty clothes lying around, magazines everywhere, etc. On the other hand, the mother explained, the girls were good students, they volunteered at a children's center, and were considerate of others, always calling home if their plans changed. But that room! The columnist wrote back - "Be grateful that you have responsible daughters, and shut the bedroom door.

So if responsibility isn't gained just by getting kids to do what they're supposed to, what *does* develop a responsible attitude? Ginott offers pages and pages of specific advice. Here's a summary of many experts' points:

Help Your Child Develop Responsibility Through:

1. Your own positive attitude towards responsibility.
2. Independence - Allowing your child to make decisions and exercise her own judgment; weigh choices and develop her own inner gauge of what's right and wrong.

3. Your sincere interest in your child's feelings will help him learn to take into consideration the feelings of others before he acts.
4. Striving for peaceful interaction by avoiding insults, name calling, threats, accusations and bossing.
5. Sensitivity - try sharing how you feel or see a situation and offering several choices of action.
6. Allowing your child to make everyday choices on behalf of the family, when appropriate.
7. Knowing when to choose for her, while helping her to accept your choices.
8. Realizing that these lessons take time and practice, everyday, in little bits of everything you do.

Getting Things Done

But, what about those tasks that have to be done while you and your kids are on the responsibility learning curve? *Stop Struggling...* authors Weinhaus and Friedman suggest cutting tasks into manageable pieces to ensure success. Instead of handing over the whole job, chunk it and use specifics. When instructing a child to clean his room, break the task out like this, for example: "First, pick up the books and put them on the shelf. Now, put the dirty clothes in this hamper. Next, put the clean clothes in the drawer. Hang your robe on the hook." And, so on.

The authors also suggest that we parents should *put the kid in charge of tasks* she alone should be handling, such as feeding her pet hermit crab, *but while offering support.* That would sound something like, "Jamie, you've been doing a fine job taking care of Hermie. Is there anything you need to keep up the good work?"

What specific responsibilities are appropriate to assign and when? What results might we hope for in return? That discussion leads us to: expectations.

Expectations

Just what should we parents expect from our kids, and how much? Progress is the *what*. The *how much* is based on a child's abilities.

Two extremes that we most often begin with are setting unreasonably high expectations or setting no expectations at all. Both efforts are bound to be ineffective set at these ends. We might feel that by not setting expectations we're making things easier by not pressuring our kids. Or, we may feel we'll miss opportunity if we don't push for the sky.   Somewhere in-between lies the correct choice for you and your child.

Educator, Leslie Nason, Ed. D., in his book *Help Your Child Succeed in School* (Cornerstone Library) reported, "Students do their best work when they know that their parents expect them to make progress and attain reasonable goals." Nason also sites that of high-school-aged students, those who are the best students know their parents expect them to go on to further education; those who are the poorest students do not. He theorized too, that students who are not doing well *could* do better if they felt that better work was really expected of them.

What about some psychologists' warnings not to push too much?   Remember, an *effective expectation focuses on progress, not perfection.* And, such an expectation should be based on a child's abilities and perhaps her interests, not on our dreams for her. For example, Nason sites that it's probably useless to expect an average child to become an aeronautical engineer if he doesn't have much science ability or interest. But, it's just as unfair to notice her flair for artistic design, then not suggest she take that extra art class. Either extreme most often may end in disappointment for parents and child. From both Ginott and Nason, unrealistic expectations can cause a child to expect too much from himself, beginning a cycle of suffering and frustration. However, if we expect far less than our child expects from herself, her self-confidence can be shaken, leading to the same cycle of suffering.

Expectations for Everyday

"But I just expect him to pick up his toys", you say. "Do I have to get into theories for that?" Weinhaus and Friedman suggest that we remember to explain two components of a task - the what and the why. The what is, describe exactly what the child is expected to do: "Pick up your toys from the floor and put them in this box." Now the trickier, why: "Toys left on the floor may get broken, or someone could fall over them and get hurt." If we expect our children to do something whether it's chores, manners, etc., it's probably not enough to say, "Because I said so." In these current times we are asking our children to question many aspects of life such as drugs, alcohol, even sex. So why should they not question even our simpler requests? We've taught them this defensive strategy, and they are practicing it. This theory is my own, you may have a different one.

When we present an expectation (teeth are to be brushed three times a day) we also can supply a reason for it (to avoid cavities, bad breath, and a big dentist bill). Now, this won't magically get the kids to do what we ask automatically, but it may be an improvement over "'Cause I'm the Momma that's why!" The key is to make sure that the reason fits the expectation - "Your job is to fill the dog's water dish at least twice a day because she'll dehydrate (or get sick for a younger child) if she doesn't have plenty of fresh water." On the other hand, "Clean your room, it's a mess" provides an unclear expectation and one person's opinion of what a mess looks like. Got it? Try it.

One other idea is to take into consideration a child's personality or learning style when asking her to follow through on a task (see Chapter Five). You may have to take him by the hand to the bathroom, put him in front of the sink with toothbrush in hand (kinesthetic). Or she may need a diagram of where to put things away (spatial), or to listen to music while working (musical). Oh, and remember to lavish on those positive comments for a job well done or even favorably attempted.

Discipline

Now that we are talking with our kids, have learned that responsibility is grown from within and that expectations must be chosen carefully, what happens when all our efforts end in rotten behavior or family feuding? While I usually pull research from a multitude of sources, again I turn to Dr. Ginott. He offers an excellent approach to discipline that seems like it could be very beneficial to our ADD kids who are often victims of their impulsive, unintentional acts.

Ginott outlines three zones of discipline, which he borrows from an analogy by Dr. Fritz Redl: green, yellow, and red zones. Yes, like a traffic light. Green is behavior that is welcome or okay. Yellow is behavior that is not okay, but can be tolerated for certain reasons. The reasons: the child is just learning, makes an honest mistake, or is in a stressful situation such as an illness, divorce or a new move. Ginott reminds us, "We don't pretend we *like* this behavior, we grant leeway because of our appreciation of hard times or new adjustments." The red zone is for conduct that cannot be tolerated and must be stopped. It should include behaviors that endanger the health and welfare of the family or its physical and financial well being (hurting others, breaking possessions). Also in the red are unacceptable behaviors due to law, ethics, or social acceptability. Ginott is firm with his list of red zone conduct. You should come up with your own list depending on your family's values and circumstances.

It would seem that just being ADD would place a child in the yellow zone for most offenses, yet over time the learning leeway is over and some yellows must turn to red. We can help by giving our child feedback on her progress. Do this by pointing out something positive first, then giving encouragement for something else he's working on. That could sound like, "Timmy, I like the way you've been keeping your hands to yourself. And, I know you're trying not to yell in the house, keep up the effort."

Limits

Now, how can we coax our kids into the green zone? Knowing what's expected can help: setting limits for them and with them is best. From an article in *Working Mother*, July/August 1996, clinical psychologist Dr. Jeffrey Chase, Ph.D. suggests establishing a few house rules that reflect your personal values (Ginott's responsibility again?): TV after homework is complete, eating is allowed only at the table, ask permission before entering another person's room, etc. "If the rule is challenged, you won't have to negotiate," says Chase. "Simply say, 'Sorry that's against house rules'" .

Ginott has something to say about limits too, plus he relates them to the discipline zones. He says limits should be stated firmly noting what is unacceptable, so the child knows you mean "red zone." And, the limit should state an acceptable substitute: "You may not punch your brother-that's red zone. You may punch your pillow in your room." Another: "You may not jump on your bed - that's red zone. You may jump outside in the yard."

Punishment

I am not even going to go to this place... Mine (and yours too, I know) are those kids who could never stay in time-out even if appropriate for their age (3 years old = 3 minutes) I spent more time chasing them back to the chair or their room. I thought about giving them an allowance so that I'd have something valuable to take away. Nah, I just try to focus on *not getting to this place.* Try the responsible attitude thing - their own guilt works wonders. Punishment options are your choice. Weigh your options carefully.

Sibling Relationships

If you have more than one child in the family you can count on sibling rivalry. They are constantly picking on each other, vying for your attention, and generally having fun that goes a bit too far. For ADD kids, a little teasing or frustration can lead to a full blown family room war. So what can we do? First, accept that sibling rivalry is a normal activity when there is more than one child in a family. The intensity of *our* children's personalities, though, tends to add heat to the flame. While most of us wouldn't dare expect "sibling harmony", we can make some positive moves toward peace. It's about kids recognizing their own and others' warning signs and knowing they have a choice in how they'll respond.

In his book mentioned earlier, *Helping Your Hyperactive Child* author Taylor stresses that we certainly cannot and should not become referees by getting in the middle of sibling skirmishes. We can and should teach our children, ADD or not, how to handle themselves. Taylor suggests promoting assertiveness by teaching children to express their feelings with words. Teach them to ask directly for what they want rather than screaming, hitting, whining, grabbing, etc.

This can be tricky with our extraordinary kids, as you might expect. So, model the behavior yourself. For example, being a control freak, I constantly have to remind myself to ease up. My kids used to run for cover when I finally "lost it". Now, I say "I feel like I'm losing control. I need someone to ...(whatever it is I need at the moment)." Try this modeling tip. Sooner or later it may work for you.

Second, help annoyed siblings learn how to handle their anger. Most anger is directed toward an unwelcome behavior, not the sibling. Using words to express feelings really can help diffuse anger. "John, I get frustrated when I'm trying to read and am constantly interrupted," may work better than "John! Stop carrying on!" This does take time and patience, but it can make a difference.

Another tip is to point out alternatives. A sibling who is feeling annoyed can at least make a choice; she can leave the room, try to get the other child to stop the annoying behavior, or agree to pay attention to the child. (Good moves for parents, too!) Knowing that they have control over their own choices can help siblings handle their anger and may be enough to diffuse an intense conflict.

Of course, there is always our attitude toward sibling rivalry - do we see it as a threat or as a necessary part of growing up? Here's one story, there are uncountable tales of siblings doing what they do best.

Beth is the mother of four children, The family's pediatrician once described the kids' rivalrous behavior: "they stimulate each other. " Beth called it hopeless, but a recent discovery changed her attitude. "I was becoming frustrated and upset by the amount and intensity of my four kids' nagging, fighting, and annoyance toward each other. My own six siblings and I drove my mother crazy and I wished my kids could have a more cordial co-existence than we did. It seemed no matter what consequences I tried, no matter how much attention I paid to them as individuals, the tension and teasing continued. Then something happened that changed my attitude about their interaction. My husband was injured in an accident at work and spent several weeks in the hospital. Between helping him and my own work, the kids spent a lot of time with a baby-sitter. Well, the reports I got back from her made me wonder if she'd been watching the wrong kids! She said they had been a joy to be with. They played games together, read to each other, even helped one another clean their rooms. So in that time of hardship, I learned that they *could* pull together and get along. That stimulation they share strengthens the sibling bond. So even though they still nag and fight and annoy, the thought that they *can and do* at times get along helps me through."

8

IT'S UP TO YOU:
YOUR JOB GUIDING YOUR ADD CHILD

At the beginning of this book I introduced the notion that in parenting ADD kids, there is a certain level of consumerism. We search for new knowledge, seek out the best programs, demand appropriate education, compare options for services, and give and seek support - in a word, we advocate.

Now that we have a base knowledge (and then some) of ADD - the what, how, why, etc., we turn to the task of advocating. Advocating doesn't have to be as serious as fighting all the way to court for educational rights, but in some cases it may lead to that. Advocating may not always be as basic as maintaining a positive attitude, but that may be the most important piece, to your child. So what does advocating involve? *Advocating includes being informed and using that information effectively on behalf of your child, other parents, and the community.* How?

Be the Most Effective Parent You Can Be

Throughout this book I've related many suggestions that we can try to be a more effective parent, such as using limits and expectations or learning to notice when we're in denial. We've discussed how to be a detective searching for the ADD diagnosis. We've talked about ways to cooperate with schools and how to help your child succeed as a student or team player. However, being an effective parent will come from within you.

While your child will benefit from the efforts you make in getting him the things he needs for success, he will grow most from your own positive attitude and, of course, unconditional love (letting him know that you love him no matter what). Granted, it's tough. That roller coaster of emotions we're riding gives us joy when our kids succeed and frustration when they fail. And not far behind all those emotions is fatigue, burn-out, weariness. At times all will seem a struggle. How can we keep up the positive face? Don't be too hard on yourself and don't give up. Remember that our kids can and do succeed, even with all their challenges. Instead of wasting your emotional energy blaming yourself for your child's struggles, remember the fact that ADD is a disability, a disorder. Then, spend that emotional energy claiming the effective attitude you have within you!

Keep Learning

After you read this book, find another dealing with ADD and read it, then another and another. Subscribe to a newsletter focusing on ADD such as those listed in the Resource Section. Attend a support meeting in your locale. Explore the Internet and find a "chat session" where you can exchange ideas with others. Whatever medium you choose, use it to continue broadening your knowledge of ADD.

Share Your Knowledge

One thing that you will get plenty of practice at is explaining ADD to other adults. Whether its teachers, coaches, or relatives, they need to understand that your child has difficulties in certain areas because her brain works differently. Remember the saying practice makes perfect? My band director in high school, Mr. Daubert, altered that fact - he said, *"Perfect practice makes perfect!"* And, believe me, you will perfect your own message about ADD that meets your needs. Some of us will share our knowledge more formally: *Attention!* magazine in its Fall 1996 issue featured an article that showcased Miss Missouri, Kimberly Massaro. Miss Massaro chose "ADD Awareness and Education" as her platform (all contestants must choose a topic to promote). Why? Her younger brother has ADD, and she wants to make a difference for people with ADD by promoting awareness and education. Share your knowledge when you need to make a difference, and you will.

Develop a Plan Of Action

A lot has been discussed in the last hundred or so pages. Your brain may be overwhelmed and you're not sure where to begin in your quest to help your child. So, we turn now to a more formal tone to begin drafting your own personal plan of action. You may already be steps ahead, but here's how to begin:

Organize Your Information

Get yourself a notebook, one that you can add pages to - a three ring binder works well. In it put plenty of note paper, some dividers with pockets, and also some clear full sheet protectors - those that hold a whole page work great. Now you have a place to put all the "stuff" that you'll come across and need to keep, and believe me you'll accumulate plenty.

Some of that stuff will include articles on ADD and other helpful topics, personal information about your child such as exam results and educational plans, dated correspondence, information to hand out to others such as teacher information or parent support topics, names, phone numbers, and addresses (of doctors, psychologists, teachers, school board member and so on), information about community resources like the United Way or Mental Health Association, and copies of state and federal laws.

Observations on the Way to Diagnosis

Notice in your child any behaviors (as listed in Chapter 2 - under "Behavioral Surveys") that are extreme. Write your observations in your notebook. Gather and compare observations made by teachers, coaches, etc. Also consider and make notes about behavioral history of family members - remember, experts do consider family history when considering low brain metabolism as the cause of ADD. Your school may provide services of a psychologist to help you gather such information, or maybe not.

Medical Exam

Next, take time to schedule a medical exam for your child to rule out illness, vision or hearing difficulties, allergies, etc. that could be causing problems. Ask the doctor for a written report.

Send in the Specialists

Specialists of all kinds can evaluate your child for emotional disorders like anxiety or family stress, other learning disabilities, or developmental delays. You'll either discover something you can treat, or you can cross another possibility off the list. You may recall that one of the best ways to a diagnosis ADD is to eliminate the possibility of other problems.

Treatment Options and Decisions

Review treatment methods that may be helpful for your particular child. Weigh the pros and cons of each treatment depending on the effects you are hoping to treat. Refer back to Chapter 4 on treatment methods and the charts on pages 62 and 63 designed to rate the severity of effects ADD has on your child. Make decisions with your child, not just for her.

Monitor and Adjust

Every month or so, revisit the original list of observations you noted about your child prior to any treatment. Gauge the effectiveness of your current treatment plan and make notes again. You will come back to compare *these* notes in about a month. Then, decide if a particular treatment needs to be adjusted, dropped, or continued as is. Keep searching for new (or renewed) treatments that might help and don't forget to share what you find.

There is a blank action plan worksheet in the Resource Section for your use.

9

TAKING CARE OF THE CARETAKER

You, You, You!

Yes, it's been you all along who has been exploring, perhaps denying, accepting and exploring again. You've fought for the right accommodation, the best programs, the least interference. You've created an environment that fosters success for your child. You are the one who's become the champion your child needs. Congratulations, champion!

And, now I am going to scold you because I know you're not taking care of yourself like you should. I know you could be giving yourself bigger breaks, you could be taking time for yourself that you so desperately need. I know *you know* what you're supposed to be doing to take care of the caretaker... So, this last chapter provides only a little on taking care of the physical and emotional you and getting and giving support. Instead, it mostly consists of reflections and quotes that might conjure up an "Aha" as you read along. The main idea is that you need to keep yourself physically strong and emotionally well so that you can continue to be that champion for your child. Here, you'll find some motivation to do what you already know. Let's go!

Health

Are you healthy? That depends on your own perception of what good health is. One perception might be a body free of illness. Another may be meeting your weight to height ratio, or maintaining your prime levels for blood pressure, cholesterol, and sugars. Good health has also been defined as a balance of body, mind , and spirit. In any case, for all you do and for all that is expected of you, you need to stay healthy. Now, that doesn't mean that you never get sick or that you'll never have a chronic condition with which to endure. We all get a cold now and then and some of us may have a mental or physical disability that challenges. But staying healthy can mean that you do what you can to *try to avoid sickness or pain*. It can mean that you follow a healthy lifestyle - focusing on a total way of living rather than an absence of illness. This is important because if you are in good health, those ills and pains won't bring us down as hard. On the other hand if we ignore our health and continue to push ourselves to meet a relentless pace, we invite illness to linger and grow - a nasty cold can turn into pneumonia in a hurry; a case of the blues into serious depression.

A healthy way of living means different things to different people, but basic components might include proper nourishment, exercise, sleep, life purpose (certain work or family care), relaxation, entertainment, and various facets of emotional and or spiritual health. When any of these components is not being satisfied, you'll surely feel the imbalance. And, your effectiveness as a parent and in other roles certainly may suffer.

Try this exercise with pencil and paper: Examine your current health balance by dividing the health pie on the next page into slices according to your own list of healthy components. The slices do not represent time in hours but should represent a level of fulfillment in relationship to the other slices.

Some examples:

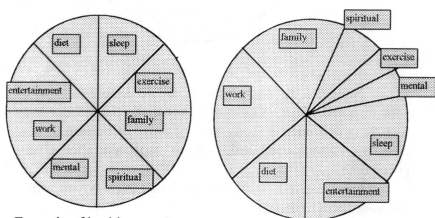

Example of health
pie in balance.

Example of health pie
out of balance.

Your turn. Divide this health pie into sections representing your particular "slices" as they are currently fulfilled.

Your current
health pie.

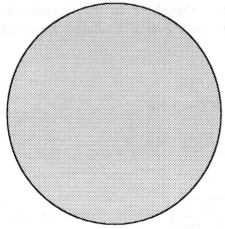

Now, you can see which "slices" need more (or less) of your time and effort. Granted, at any given time in our lives something or someone needs more of us. Just be sure to take time to rebalance your health efforts, especially after a very giving time.

Next, create a health pie that looks the way you would like your slices to appear:

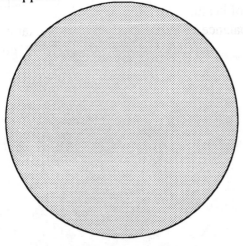

Your health
pie as you'd
like it to be.

Emotional Wellness

As you consider the state of your emotional wellness, be mindful to notice your feelings. We're all angry, worried, concerned, or something else at some point. However, our wellness depends on how we handle those emotions. Know that your moods can have an effect on your child, too. Many ADD kids are very sensitive - it's part of their nature - and they tend to let our attitudes affect them, often giving back the same emotions that we give out (some clinicians call it reactive behavior). It works both ways, too. Are you a person who lets your kids' moods affect *you?* I know I fall into that pattern easily, so I have to step away for a moment if I can't resist the reactive effect.

What can we do if we just can't seem to deal with all these emotions? Talk to someone, whether it's a counselor, your doctor, or a friend. Dealing with ADD takes an enormous effort, and sometimes you will need to rely on professional help. Call your mental health association for direction; there are many options like group sessions, private counseling and phone hot-lines. Perhaps you're a very private person and are uncomfortable sharing with others. A good counselor can teach you methods that can relieve stress such as relaxation techniques or, my favorite, writing in a personal journal.

Journal writing has become popular in the last few years. There are seminars on how to do it and most book stores offer a wide variety of journals to record your thoughts from paperback to leather bound. A friend of mine uses a 5" x 9" size that is covered in denim. A business associate has extra pages in his appointment book. Another uses her notebook computer to record her thoughts; I suspect striking the keys is part of the release for her as well. Any medium will do, it has to be comfortable for you. Furthermore, you don't have to keep what you write. A parent in an ADD support group noted that he writes things on any paper scrap that's handy, even napkins, and then he crumbles it up and shoots for the garbage can. Very therapeutic, he says!

Getting and Giving Support

Sometimes we may not need the formality of professional guidance, but just a little support from a good ally. Just what is support? It could be an encouraging word that eases our mind, some information we need for a teacher, a couple hours baby-sitting, or whatever else helps us endure our frustrations and maintain our efforts. Many of us find it difficult to ask for any type of help, and asking for support is not easy. Getting it is easier. Try to remember that there are allies out there who are ready and willing to support you. You've been there for others needing a nudge, and they'll be there for you, too. It's a part of advocating, really. Get in touch with a fellow ADD parent, attend a parents' meeting at school or in the community. Hang around the gym while your kids have basketball practice and chat with the other moms and dads.

In giving support to someone who finds it hard to ask for help, be a good listener and ask questions. You'll find that other people love to talk about themselves and their kids. And by asking questions you can keep any whining or bragging to a minimum....*I see that your son is very athletic, what is his favorite sport?* • *Yes, girls can be nasty to each other at this age, what activities does she keep busy with?* • *Oh, it is tough to get the right help for slow readers, what programs are they using at your school?* • *Yes, my daughter is very active also, do your teachers use any special techniques in class?* And, so on.

Reflections

This section is certainly a joy to share. To me, there's nothing like good reading, especially when some passage or idea hits you between the eyes and you say to yourself, *Aha! How true.* I hope you'll find some ahas in the words ahead.

Do not free a camel of the burden of his hump. You may be freeing him from being a camel.
-G.K. Chesterton

My mother had a great deal of trouble with me, but I think she rather enjoyed it.
-Mark Twain

...if you're alive, you got to flap your arms and legs, you got to jump around a lot, you got to make a lot of noise, because life is the very opposite of death. And therefore, as I see it, if you're quiet, you're not living. You've got to be noisy, or at least your thoughts should be noisy and colorful and lively.
-Mel Brooks

I have found the best way to give advice to your children is to find out what they want and then advise them to do it.
-Harry S. Truman

Everything in moderation, including moderation.
-Jack Kornfield, Buddhist teacher

Childhood is not an easy time. I feel sorry for children who are raised by those who take no responsibility for parenting. We must spread the good word about the rewards of being a responsible parent.
-Art Linkletter

You miss 100% of the shots you never take.
-Wayne Gretsky

If A equals success, then the formula is $A = X + Y + Z$. Where X is work, Y is play, and Z is keeping your mouth shut.
-Albert Einstein

We don't have to be perfect parents, just good enough ones.
-ADD Parent

You cannot put the same shoe on every foot.
-Publilius Syrus

One of the secrets of a happy life is continuous small treats.
-Iris Murdoch

Figure out what you can fix and what you can't fix, and do something nice for yourself.
-ADD Parent

Start by doing what's necessary; then do what's possible; and suddenly you are doing the impossible.
- St. Francis of Assisi

Education is what survives when what has been learnt has been forgotten.
-B.F. Skinner

Progress always involves risk. You can't steal second base and keep your foot on first.
-Frederick B. Wilcox

It is always possible to approach a goal by a detour.
-Theodore Reik
No one can make you feel inferior without your consent.
-Eleanor Roosevelt

If your compassion does not include yourself, it is incomplete.
-Jack Kornfield, Buddhist teacher

Raising these kids is a challenge and a wonder- a sense of humor is the only saving grace for me sometimes.
-ADD Parent

Grant that I may not so much seek to be consoled as to console; to be understood as to understand; to be loved as to love ...
-St. Francis of Assisi

Remember that YOU are the most important person in your life right now. If you are not healthy and together, you cannot help your child. Take very good care of yourself.
-ADD Parent

Making the things you do every day as beautiful as possible is a way to live a happy life.
-Alexandra Stoddard

Advice is what we ask for when we already know the answer but wish we didn't.
-Erica Jong

I learned to lighten up on those things that just do not make a whole lot of difference.
-ADD Parent

The average mom who holds a job outside the home works an 84-hour week to meet her responsibilities at work and at home.
-PR Reporter

Don't argue about difficulties. The difficulties will argue for themselves.
-Winston Churchill

One can never consent to creep when one feels an impulse to soar.
-Helen Keller

In the beginner's mind there are many possibilities, in the expert's mind there are few.
-Shunryu Suzuki, Buddhist Scholar

Children internalize their parents' unhappiness. Fortunately they absorb our contentment just as readily.
-Lucille Ball

The best advice I ever came across on the subject of concentration is: "Wherever you are, be there."
-Jim Rohn

I've been on a calendar, but I've never been on time.
-Marilyn Monroe

To change and change for the better are two different things.
-German Proverb

A proverb is a short sentence based on long experience.
-Miguel de Cervantes

I know God will not give me anything I can't handle. I just wish He didn't trust me so much.
-Mother Teresa

In the final analysis it is not what you do for your children but what you have taught them to do for themselves that will make them successful human beings.
-Ann Landers

Only the inquiring mind solves problems.
-Edward Hodnett

Not one of us has a blank page in the books of the Recording Angel.
-George Bernard Shaw

He that will make a good use of any part of his life must allow a large part of it for recreation.
-John Locke

Any activity becomes creative when the doer cares about doing it right, or better.
-John Updike

What you need to do is investigate all the options and figure out which is the best option for your kid.
-ADD Parent

The essential conditions of everything you do must be choice, love, passion.
-Nadia Boulanger

Reflect upon your present blessings, of which every man has many; not on your past misfortunes, of which all men have some.
-Charles Dickens

In the long run, we shape our lives, and we shape ourselves. The process never ends until we die. And the choices we make are ultimately our own responsibility.
-Eleanor Roosevelt

Inch by inch, everything's a cinch.
-Dr. Robert Schuller

Tact is the knack of making a point without making an enemy.
-Howard W. Newton

You teach best what you most need to learn.
-Richard Bach

When you row another person across the river, you get there yourself.
-Anonymous

A problem is a chance for you to do your best.
-Duke Ellington

Imagination is more important than knowledge.
-Albert Einstein

On argument: *The thing to do is supply light and not heat.*
-Woodrow Wilson

If you have never been hated by your child, you have never been a parent.

-Bette Davis

It's amazing how much ruckus a single kid can cause.
-ADD Parent

There is very little difference in people, but that little difference makes a big difference. The little difference is attitude. The big difference is whether it is positive or negative.
-Clement Stone

Many of life's failures are people who did not realize how close they were to success when they gave up.
-Thomas Edison

Knowledge is the antidote of fear.
-William Brady

There is more to life than increasing its speed.
-Gandhi

The rules of life are found within yourself. Ask yourself constantly, "What is the right thing to do?"
-Confucius

Every horse thinks his pack heavy.
-German Saying

I don't want the cheese, I just want to get out of the trap.
-Spanish Proverb

The last of the human freedoms - to choose one's attitude in any given set of circumstances, to choose one's own way.
-Victor Frankl

Pick battles big enough to matter, small enough to win.
-Jonathon Kozol

It is part of the cure to want to be cured.
-Seneca
Why do birds sing in the morning? It's the triumphant shout: "We got through another night."
-Enid Bagnold

Only those who will risk going too far can possibly find out how far one can go.
-T.S. Eliot

When angry, count ten before you speak; if very angry, an hundred.
-Abraham Lincoln

In all our efforts to provide "advantages" we have actually produced the busiest, most competitive, highly pressured and over-organized generation of youngsters in our history—and possibly the unhappiest. We seem hell-bent on eliminating much of childhood.
-Eda J. Le Shan

Once you bring life into the world, you must protect it. We must protect it by changing the world.
-Elie Wiesel

We're all in this alone.
-Lily Tomlin

I am not an adventurer by choice but by fate.
-Vincent Van Gogh

And that's the way it is
-Walter Cronkite

Resource Section

Associations and Support Groups

American Academy of Pediatrics Division of Publications
141 Northwest Point Blvd.
PO Box 927
Elk Grove Village, IL 60009 0927
Write for: *Understanding the ADHD Child*

Attention Deficit Disorders Association (ADDA)
12345 Jones Road
Suite 287
Houston, TX 77070
(713) 955-3720

Children and Adults with Attention Deficit Disorders
(CHADD) National Headquarters
499 NW 70th Avenue
Plantation FL 33317
(305) 587-3700

Learning Disabilities Association (LDA)
4156 Library Road
Pittsburgh, PA 15234
(412) 341-1515

National Attention Deficit Disorder Assoc. (ADDA)
9930 Johnnycake Ridge Road - Suite 3E
Mentor , OH 44060
1-800-487-2282 fax back (313) 769-6729 http://www.add.org

Dr. Nancy O'Dell / Dr. Patricia Cook
School of Education, University of Indianapolis
1400 East Hanna Avenue
Indianapolis, Indiana 46227-3679

National Center for Learning Disabilities
99 Park Avenue
New York, NY 10016
(212) 687-7211

National Information Center for Children and Youth with Disabilities (NICHCY)
PO Box 1492
Washington, DC 20013 1492
1-800-695-0285

Parent Education Network
333 East 7th Avenue
York, PA 17404
(717) 845-9722

Further Reading

Books

Arnold, M., & Novick, B. (1995). *Why Is My Child Having Trouble at School?* G.P. Putnam's Sons

Friedman, K., & Weinhaus, E. (1991). *Stop Struggling with Your Child.* Harper Perennial

Ginott, H. (1965). *Between Parent and Child: New Solutions to Old Problems.* The Macmillan Company

Goldstein, S., & Ingersoll, B. (1993). *Attention Deficit Disorder and Learning Disabilities: Realities, Myths, and Controversial Treatments.* A Main Street Book / Doubleday

Greenspan, S., *The Challenging Child:* Addison-Wesley, 1995

Hartmann, T. (1993). *Attention Deficit Disorder: A Different Perception.* Underwood Books

Levine, M. (1990). *Keeping A Head In School: A Student's Book About Learning Abilities & Learning Disorders.* Educators Publishing Service, Inc.

Levinson, H. (1990). *Total Concentration.* M. Evans & Company, Inc.

McWilliams, P. & Roger, J. (1991) *Life 101.* Prelude Press, Inc.

Montapert, A. (1986) *Words of Wisdom to Live By* Books Of Value

Microsoft Bookshelf (©1987 - 1995) Microsoft Corporation

Nason, L. (no date). *Help Your Child Succeed In School.* Cornerstone Library

Reif, S. (1993). *How to Reach and Teach ADD/ADHD Children: Practical Techniques, Strategies, and Interventions for Helping Children with Attention Problems and Hyperactivity.* The Center for Applied Research in Education

Stoddard, A. (1995) *The Art of the Possible: The path from perfectionism to balance and freedom.* William Morrow Co, Inc.

Wodrich, D. (1994) *Attention Deficit Hyperactivity Disorder: What Every Parent Wants to Know:* Brookes Publishing Co.

Publications

The ADDed Line
3320 Creek Hollow Drive
Marietta, GA 30062
1-800-982-4028

Attention! & *Chadder Box* & *CHADD FACTS*
(CHADD) National Headquarters
499 NW 70th Avenue
Plantation FL 33317
(305) 587-3700

Challenge
PO Box 488
West Newbury, MA 01985-1214
(518) 462-0495

Champion: Mastering the ADD Challenge
JMA Publications
PO Box 1127
Lebanon PA 17042 1127
(717) 228-2302 / janemiller@msn.com

Internet Sources

AskERIC - The federal Educational Resources Information Center http://ericir.syr.edu/

CH.A.D.D - Children and Adults with Attention Deficit Disorders http://www.chadd.org/

ADDA Home Page - National Attention Deficit Disorder Association   http://www.add.org

Disability-Specific Web Sites

http://www.disserv.stu.umn.edu/disability/Learning_Disabilities/

EdLaw Home Page
   http://www.access.digex.net:80/~edlawinc/

Learning Disabilities Resources
   http://www.byu.edu/acd1/ed/coe/vlibrary/ld.html

The Neurological Bases of Attention Deficit Disorder
   http://www.generation.net/~dieter/adhd.html

Pharmacy Information Network Drug Database
   http://Pharminfo.com/drugdb/db_mnu.html

Special Education Resources on the Internet (SERI)
   http://www.hood.edu/seri/serihome.htm

Some Commercial Internet Providers

America On Line
1-800-218-5454

CompuServe
1-800-487-0588

Microsoft Network (MSN)
1-800-386-5550

Check your local yellow pages or business directory for Internet providers in your area

Products

ADDvance Publications
57 Hale RD Wembley Downs
Perth, Western Australia 6019
(09) 385-9250
fax requests for catalog (09) 385-9252
from US dial 011-619-385-9252

A.D.D. WareHouse
1-800-233-9273 (for catalog)

GSI Publications, Inc.
(315) 446-4849 (for catalog)

Samples

Sample Conners' Teachers' Questionnaire

Child_____Grade_____
Date_____

Answer all questions. Beside each item, indicate the degree of
the problem by a check mark ☑.

	0	1	2	3
	Not at all	Just a little	Pretty much	Very much
1. Restless or overactive				
2. Excitable, impulsive				
3. Disturbs other children				
4. Fails to finish things started				
5. Easily frustrated				
6. Inattentive, easily distracted				
etc.				

Scale items used with permission of Multi-Health Systems, Inc. 908
Niagara Falls Blvd. N Tonawanda, NY 14120-2060 (1-800-456-3003)

Note: Such questionnaires are designed to collect information from
school and at home as different environments can influence ratings.
You can create your own questionnaire by listing behaviors noted
from the **DSM IV-R** beginning on page 25. Then rate for either
environment. A clinician can convert the ratings to scores to assist in
diagnosis and treatment plans. A blank questionnaire follows.

Your Child Needs A Champion

Sample questionnaire for rating degree of behaviors.

Child_____Age_____

Date_____

Enter behaviors from the APA listing beginning on page 25. Beside each item, indicate the degree of the problem by a check mark ✔.

	0	1	2	3
	Not at all	Just a little	Pretty much	Very much

The APA reminds us not to use the list of behaviors from the *Diagnostic and Statistical Manual, 4th Edition (DSM IV-R)*, as the sole tool for diagnosis. The list should be used with careful developmental history and observation to define a general pattern of behavior.

Your Child Needs A Champion

Sample Action Plan Work Sheet

(You will want to create one page for each of these sections.   This worksheet gets you started.)

How will I Organize My Information

Observations of _____ **on the Way to Diagnosis**
                              (child's name)

Medical Exam (Date, Doctor Name, Questions…)

Sample Action Plan Worksheet (cont.)

Specialists (Therapists, counselors, etc.)

Treatment Options and Decisions

Monitor and Adjust

Glossary

(As relating to ADD)

attention- the ability to concentrate, having ability to receive stimuli and select focus.

acceptance- the act of thinking of as usual, correct, true or satisfactory.

accomodate- to assist, to provide a favorable situation.

adapt- to change so as to be suitable for a different condition or purpose.

accountable- to be responsible for

attitude- disposition or temperament, one's nature or opinion towards life.

behavior modification- an effort that strives to change a resulting behavior.

caretaker- a person engaged to take care of loved ones precious to another

champion- to fight for or defend a cause or movement; a person who does so.

consequence- natural or logical outcomes of behavior, something that happens as a result of some other action or condition.

cure- a treatment that makes an ill person well or a disorder go away, a return to good health

CVS- cerebral vestibular system; a system of the brain that regulates certain functions

deficit- a lack of something needed

denial- disbelief, the act of thinking as untrue or not usual

discipline- training of the mind, body or character that demands obedience and self-control

disorder- an ailment or sickness, a hardship or state of trouble

distractibility- being drawn away or having attention diverted

expectation- a hope or prospect, anticipated result

exploration- the act of searching

hyperactivity- showing an unusual amount of activity, excess energy

IDEA- Individuals with Disabilities Education Act, IDEA and its amendments mandates minimum requirements for free appropriate public education of children and youth with disabilities

IEP- Individualized Education Plan, a plan that addresses academic and behavioral issues

impulsivity- behavior of acting "on a whim" without thinking, having weak impulse control

inattentive- being unavailable to external stimuli, inability to select what to focus on, inability to filter too much stimuli

limit- a boundary or point which we are not to surpass, an extent to which we may venture

neurobiological- related to the brain and body

*neurotransmitter-*naturally occurring chemical messenger that works in the brain

PL- public law

punishment- penalty for wrongdoing

recycling- revisiting past levels of awareness, going through stages of old feelings and thoughts again

responsibility- quality of meeting duties, being reliable, dependable

self-esteem- one's thoughts about oneself, level of respect and honor for oneself

passion- great enthusiasm, a powerful feeling

success- achievement of some desired thing

Index

Notes

Every effort has been made to appropriately credit the copyright owners of material quoted in this reference. If any sources have not been sufficiently credited, please contact the publisher and efforts will be made to correct in subsequent printings.

This reference is based on the author's personal experience with and research of ADD. Contents are not intended to replace medical and/or psychological diagnosis or treatment of ADD. Readers should consult a qualified physician or health care professional in matters related to physical and mental health. This reference is not to be considered as medical advice.

Acknowledgments

Cassie Lynn Miller
You challenge me, my love. Your enthusiasm and curiosity are treasures. I love you!

Joey Miller, III
I just can't keep up with you, but I will always try! Remember who taught you to hit a baseball (*not* your Uncle) - I love you!

Paul Moceri, PCS
You were the first to help me learn about ADD as I searched for help for my family. Thank you.

All the teachers and staff at OLV
You are all so committed to the children, and to mine especially it seems. Bless you!

Dave Sabo, Ph.D.
You inspired me with your words, "Don't discount the amazing ability children have to self-monitor - to 'catch themselves'- concerning their behaviors and feelings."

To all the parents who offered their stories so that we all can seek to understand. Your sharing has been gracious.

Mom & Dad
Thanks for your faith in me and the kids.

Joe Miller, Jr.
My husband, I didn't mention you at all, okay? I love you!

About the Author

Jane Miller, ADD Mom, first learned (the truth) about ADD when trying desperately to help her struggling first grade daughter. After two years and considerable effort, she called upon what she had learned to help her struggling first grade *son*. Ms. Miller currently assists others in learning about and mastering the ADD challenge through writing and speaking, drawing from her personal knowledge and understanding. She has over twelve years experience in public relations and marketing, is an approved professional development consultant and a certified facilitator in the areas of corporate change and personal growth. Ms. Miller resides with her husband and two children in Lebanon, Pennsylvania.

For a sample newsletter or for information on seminars and speaking engagements, contact:

newsletter:
Champion: Mastering the ADD Challenge
JMA Publications
PO Box 1127
Lebanon PA 17042 1127
(717) 228-2302 / janemiller@msn.com

seminars/speaking engagements:
Jane Miller & Associates
PO Box 1127
Lebanon PA 17042 1127
(717) 228-2302 / janemiller@msn.com
Web Page http://SwiftSite.com/ADDChampion

Yes! Please send me the following items from the AD/HD CHAMPION Series: (ALL US SHIPPING INCLUDED!)

		qty	price
BOOK: Your Child Needs A Champion @ 19.95 5 ½ x 8 ½ over 210 pages!		___	_____
NEWSLETTER: AD/HD Champion @ 10.00 6 issues. At least 6 pages every issue!		___	_____
BOOKLET: Practical Tips for Mastering *AD/HD Everyday* @ 6.50		___	_____
BOOKLET: *Champion Parents Coping* *Guide: Nurturing Your Spirit Everyday* @ 6.50		___	_____

PA residents add 6% sales tax on products.
($1.00 on book, .60 on newsletter, .30 on booklets)   PA Tax   _____

Overseas Orders please add air mail costs   Airmail   _____
($ 8.00 Book, $ 3.00 booklet, $ 2.00 newsletter)

TOTAL   [   ]

Check_____   Money Order_____   *(payable to Miller & Associates)*

VISA_____   MasterCard_____
For charge purchases please enter account number:

_ _ _ _   _ _ _ _   _ _ _ _   exp. date _____

signature _____

Charge Orders may be mailed or:
faxed to 717-228-2302, e-mailed to janemiller@msn.com
or submitted on our home page at
http://SwiftSite.com/ADDChampion

Miller & Associates
PO Box 1127
Lebanon PA 17042

Name _____

Address _____

City_____ State_____ Zip _____

Thank You for your order !

Yes! Please send me the following items from the AD/HD CHAMPION Series: <u>(ALL US SHIPPING INCLUDED!)</u>

	qty	price
BOOK: *Your Child Needs A Champion* @ *19.95*	____	_____
5 ½ x 8 ½ over 210 pages!		
NEWSLETTER: AD/HD Champion @ *10.00*	____	_____
6 issues. At least 6 pages every issue!		
BOOKLET: *Practical Tips for Mastering*		
AD/HD Everyday @ *6.50*	____	_____
BOOKLET: *Champion Parents Coping*		
Guide: Nurturing Your Spirit Everyday @ *6.50*	____	_____

PA residents add 6% sales tax on products.
($1.00 on book, .60 on newsletter, .30 on booklets)   PA Tax _____

Overseas Orders please add air mail costs   Airmail _____
($ 8.00 Book, $ 3.00 booklet, $ 2.00 newsletter)
TOTAL [   ]

Check_____   Money Order_____ (*payable to Miller & Associates*)

VISA_____   MasterCard_____
For charge purchases please enter account number:

_ _ _ _ _ _ _ _ _ _ _ _   exp. date _____

signature _____
Charge Orders may be mailed or:
faxed to 717-228-2302, e-mailed to janemiller@msn.com
or submitted on our home page at
http://SwiftSite.com/ADDChampion

Miller & Associates
PO Box 1127
Lebanon PA 17042

Name _____

Address _____

City_____ State_____ Zip _____

Thank You for your order !

Your Child Needs A Champion

Your Child Needs A Champion